D0914344

For Joseph Palladino
Thank you for coming
Pete Weisbrod
2/90

"I dreamed last night we were together...
I dream about you often...
But worst of all I dreamed you died."

Mary McAdam

SUICIDE:
SURVIVORS

WHAT PROFESSIONALS SAY:

"I thought I would just peruse the manuscript of **SUICIDE: SURVIVORS**, but I couldn't put it down. It's written with extraordinary sensitivity and insight; the reader will find a wealth of practical wisdom in this poignant and indispensable book." Dr. Earl Grollman, Rabbi, Belmont, MA — Speaker and author.

"**SUICIDE: SURVIVORS** is filled with a great deal of experientially based wisdom. Wisdom, for me, is much more than knowledge...Your sharing of your own pain and empathetic understanding of the needs of other suicide survivors is extremely helpful because you go beyond knowledge to wisdom." Paul E. Irion, Millersville, PA — Religious consultant to the National Funeral Director's Ass'n.

"**SUICIDE: SURVIVORS** is clearly written, sensitive and an extremely helpful volume... written by someone who has experienced the pain herself...The humanity and warmth that characterized Ms. Wrobleski's earlier work is seen again...It is a book that provides hope and and reassurance." Andrew Slaby, M.D., Ph.D, M.P.H., Summit, NJ — 1990–1991 President of the American Ass'n of Suicidology.

"**SUICIDE: SURVIVORS** is a long over-due book. It offers explanations, education, comfort and hope...It goes into concerns not addressed in other books...The book contains insights into why or what may have contributed to the death. A terrific book that will be more helpful to suicide survivors than any book I have read." Helen Fitzgerald, Springfield, VA, Coordinator, Grief Program, Mt Vernon Center.

SUICIDE:
SURVIVORS

A GUIDE FOR THOSE LEFT BEHIND

SUICIDE: SURVIVORS

A GUIDE FOR THOSE LEFT BEHIND

DAVID L. RICE LIBRARY
UNIVERSITY OF SOUTHERN INDIANA
EVANSVILLE, IN

Adina Wrobleski
AFTERWORDS PUBLISHING
Minneapolis, Minnesota

23943016

Copyright © 1991 by Adina Wrobleski
Published by:

Adina Wrobleski
AFTERWORDS PUBLISHING
5124 Grove Street Minneapolis, MN 55436
(612)929-6448

Printed in the United States of America
First Edition 1991

All rights reserved. No part of this book may be reproduced in any form
or by any means without permission in writing from the publisher.

PUBLISHERS CATALOGING IN PUBLICATION DATA

Wrobleski, Adina Suicide: Survivors — A Guide for Those Left Behind
   1. Suicide — North America 2. Mental Illness. 3. Psychiatry.
   4. Psychology. I. Title.

Library of Congress Catalog Card Number: 91-71127

ISBN 0-935585-04-4

FOR ALL MY FRIENDS IN SA\VE

Faye Bland, Karen Deviny, Mary and Al Kluesner,
Reuel Nygaard, Bonnie Scherer, Mary Swanson,
Nancy Theis, Ben Van Sant, and Ron and Marian Weiss.

TABLE OF CONTENTS

About the Author

Adina Wrobleski is an internationally recognized authority on suicide and grief after suicide. She helps people understand that suicide is not a bewildering mystery that cannot be understood. There is a worldwide body of science about suicide, and her specialty is taking complicated psychiatric and psychological evidence, and explaining it in clear and interesting language through writing and speaking.

This is the second book Adina Wrobleski has written. Her first book **SUICIDE: WHY? — 85 Questions and Answers About Suicide** was the culmination of her quest for information about suicide that was lacking in 1979 when her twenty-one-year-old daughter, Lynn, killed herself.

SUICIDE: SURVIVORS — A Guide for Those Left Behind reflects Wrobleski's personal experience of suicide grief and recovery. She extends her hand to new suicide survivors, and gives them guideposts, reassurance, information, comfort, and hope.

ACKNOWLEDGMENTS

I am very grateful to the following people who read and critiqued this book in manuscript. Their help, encouragement and kind words improved this book, and meant more to me than I can say. They are: Lee Beecher, MD; Catherine Carson; Wilma Carry; Helen Fitzgerald; Rabbi Earl Grollman; Ron Hunter; Paul Irion; Bonnie Scherer; Andrew Slaby, MD, PhD, MPH; Mary L. Sulesky (Hermitage, PA); Mary L. Sulesky (Arlington, VA); Mary Swanson; Joseph H. Talley, MD; and Al and Linda Vigil.

I especially want to thank my friend and editor, Ravina Gelfand. I also appreciate the help and friendship of Bob Morris and Ed Wedman. I thank my husband, Henry Wrobleski, who has supported and encouraged me to continue in what has been a long journey.

PREFACE

A suicide survivor is any person grieving a suicide death. (Suicide attempters are people who have attempted, but not completed suicide.) **SUICIDE: SURVIVORS** is a personal message from Adina Wrobleski to survivors. **SUICIDE: SURVIVORS** gives friends and professionals a look at the world of pain survivors inhabit.

There are some fine books written for suicide survivors, but **SUICIDE: SURVIVORS** is unique in its detailing of what survivors can expect on their road through grief and recovery. They will be reassured by the fact that someone they have never met can describe what they are experiencing.

SUICIDE: SURVIVORS is practical. It speaks to common problems of survivors, offers advice, gives solutions that have worked for others, and above all it offers encouragement and hope.

Minneapolis, Minnesota September 1991

PROLOGUE

About 6:30 on the evening of August 16, 1979, my husband Hank and I were feeling particularly happy. It had been a nice day, and we had just finished dinner dishes when the doorbell rang. Since my husband had been a police officer for thirty years, we smiled when we saw a uniformed policeman at our door — he was a friend.

We knew him well and were glad to see him, so it took a bit of time for him to get our attention. And then he told us — just the bare facts the Lakeville police had given him "I have bad news; your daughter Lynn is dead. She shot herself." Her husband had found her body around 4:00 P.M.

Physical shock is an interesting phenomenon. It is the mind's way of anesthetizing us from pain, and it lets in reality in small doses, enabling us to do what has to be done. (It causes people to say of us, "My, how well they are doing.")

Hank's first impulse was to go to the town where she lived with her husband. But first we had to call Lynn's brother Joe and her sister Dawn, as well as my sisters and brother. It was a terrible night. We couldn't reach Dawn because she travels, and we had to ask our local police department to request the Bangor, Maine police to find and tell Joe. He called three times that night to convince himself it was true.

The next morning, through her work in Washington, D.C., we found out where Dawn was. She had a double shock because the message I left at her work to "call her father" got changed to "call home," and she thought that Hank had died. As her relief flooded in about Hank, she had to absorb the blow that Lynn had died.

We did drive the twenty miles to Lynn's home that night, and then back to our home to make the calls to our relatives and friends. We told them what we knew: Lynn was dead; she had shot herself.

THE FUNERAL

The rest of the funeral experiences were the same, probably, as all bereaved people suffer. We were lucky because Joe and Dawn were able to stay for two weeks. But then they were gone, and we were on our own.

In the next months we discovered what a blessing shock really is. The heavy numbing, zombie-like shock of the first few days gradually lifts. But it stays a long time, enabling one — most of the time — to go through the motions of returning to ordinary life.

WHAT HAPPENED?

So what happened to Lynn? It was so clear afterwards. I divide the last eight years of her life into the bad five years, and the good three years. Lynn was a "terrible kid," and we had a lot of what we thought were behavior problems with her. That's what the counselors and therapists told us. And I was a "terrible mother" too. I was punitive and angry, and she and I had a lot of power fights. Often Hank was in the middle. There were a lot of good times, but her junior and senior high school years were marked by anxiety, frustration and anger for all of us.

Lynn refused to go to school much of the time, and often would sleep until five o'clock in the afternoon. We now know that this excessive sleeping was one symptom of her deep depression. So were most of the other things she did. She was sick, and we didn't know it!

She was defiant, rebellious and disobedient. It was about her junior year in high school — after trying punishment, bribery, incentives, and periodic counseling — that we gave up and just let her run. She was doing poorly in school, doing everything she could to push our buttons, and was completely out of our control. She got jobs and quit or was fired. We were fortunate that she was never promiscuous, on drugs, or in trouble with the law.

In the middle of her senior year, she moved out, and truthfully, we were relieved. She had met her future husband. They soon bought a house, and somewhere along the way she and I forgave each other. Through the bad five years (when she lived at home), our love for each other stayed alive, and in the good three years (after she moved), we often talked about the "bad" years. She used to laugh and say, "The way for kids to learn to get along with their mother is to move out." It's not good advice, but it worked for us. She and I began to develop a true mother-daughter relationship.

THE NEW BEGINNING

I remember when it started. She had just been gone a couple of days when the phone rang. I answered and it was Lynn. She wanted to know, "How do you make pot roast?" She always adored her father, but now our love began to grow deeper — phone calls — meeting her for lunch — she dropped by our house. Occasionally, the four of us got together. Lynn seemed happy and busy all the time.

Only after she died did we remember the annoyance we felt when she called us and there were long silences on her part. She said something, we replied, and then silence. She was reaching out to us; she wanted something, but she couldn't tell us what it was, nor do I think she knew. We forgot these awkward conversations after we hung up.

Also, twice in the months before her death, she came over wanting reassurance. Once she was frightened about predictions by evangelists that the world was coming to an end. The other time, she was worried whether we would go to war with Russia. (This kind of 'eschatological' thinking is frequently found in mental illness.)

THE WEDDING

It was 1977, and Lynn was nineteen, and suddenly (it seemed), we were planning her wedding — that whole bit that mothers and daughters do. And it was a lovely wedding. We did something fun. We left all the presents unopened, and the day after the wedding they came over, along with her mother-in-law, and Dawn and Joe, and we had a big party opening the presents. The last two gifts were from us — completing her china and tableware to eight settings. The day after they got back from their honeymoon, they came over with a gift to thank us for the wedding.

Lynn's depression had lifted, and she seemed happy for the first time in years. Her father said afterwards, "I had always worried about her — both consciously and unconsciously — until she got married. Then I thought she turned the corner." (I think she lived three years longer than she would have if she hadn't met her husband.)

Our relationship grew. She was a great one for sending cards — whether there was an occasion or not. For an event, she usually sent two cards. I'll never forget the first time she sent me flowers on Mother's Day. A couple of days after she died, I came home and saw all the flowers our friends had sent, and in my fog, thought: "That's funny. The only one who ever sends me flowers is Lynn." Then reality crashed around me again.

Lynn occasionally bought me small presents, but most importantly, we continued talking, doing things and growing together. Where had this beautiful, thoughtful young woman come from? I never clearly felt — except for those last three years — the joy and pride of mothers as they see bits and pieces of themselves reflected in their daughters. I recalled all those years she fought me, and I fought her — trying to instill my standards, tastes, ideas and practices. She had heard me. In those three years I saw things in Lynn that she could only have learned from me.

And they were achieving so much! Lynn was a driver — we thought then; now we think she was driven. They bought a lovely home, but almost as soon as they had it, Lynn wanted to build their dream house. She was only twenty years old, and her husband a year older. Maybe she knew her time was short. They bought and sold nine acres for a homesite that didn't work out. We hoped she would stop her search for awhile, but back out she went looking for the perfect site. And she found it; twenty acres in the country.

A FRENZIED TIME

Looking back, it was a frenzied time. She did all the running to courthouses, lawyers, contractors and banks. She was working too. We shopped for carpet and curtains and tile. Their new house was a month away from completion when she killed herself. She was twenty-one-years-old, and she had everything going for her. But she also had a brain disease called major depression, and the way one dies from depression is by suicide.

Figuratively, I think that Lynn kept all her pain and anger behind a locked door which she kept closed through sheer strength all her life. I think that about three months before she died, that door started opening. She forced it shut again, and went about picking out the furnishings for her new home. But it kept opening, and she had to use more and more of her diminishing strength to keep that door to death closed.

THE NEW HOUSE

About three weeks before Lynn's death there came a key danger sign which no one understood. I saw it two days before she died, and didn't understand it. The big, unrecognized signal she gave was a complete reversal in her feelings about something she cared for. She suddenly hated, feared and felt hopeless about their new house. This was the house she was a month away from moving into — her dream house.

Her husband saw another abrupt change. She had loved horses since her childhood, and as soon as they bought their first house, Lynn finally got her own horse. About three months before she died, she suddenly and abruptly lost all interest in Roxanne. She took care of her, but she didn't ride or enjoy Roxanne any more.

People have asked me, "Didn't her husband see any signs?" And I reply, "Of course he did," as do all survivors after a suicide. At the time we didn't know what we were seeing, and were too afraid to look. One gets awfully smart about suicide after it happens, and a lot of things are clear then. But to a young man working eighteen hours a day, and trying to figure out what has made such changes in his wife, it is not clear. As bad as it was for us, I felt horror at her husband being a twenty-two-year-old widower!

I didn't see any really visible tearfulness and dejection in Lynn until two days before her death. She called me in the morning of August 14, and I met her for lunch. We talked for four hours. Instead of taking her to a hospital emergency room, because she was near death, I reasoned with her.

I knew and recognized then that she was depressed, and even talked to her about it. I knew in the back of my mind that there is something called major depression — a serious brain disease — but in my great wisdom, I thought she had the "ordinary" kind of bad mood most of us experience — the kind one "gets over" or "comes out of."

Mostly we talked about the house that day — of how to cope with living there when she didn't want to — because she had to live in the house at least until they could sell it. I told her she had no other alternative, but Lynn knew that she did.

She had cheered up when she left, and I did too, assuming the crisis had passed. When we were waiting at the cash register, she put her arms around me and said, "Thanks for caring." I told her I loved her, and she told me she loved me too. Her husband later said she came home feeling optimistic, and had discussed with him what she and I had talked about. But she couldn't hold on to it. She called me three times the next day wanting to hear again some point we had talked about. She was having a very hard time concentrating.

THE END

The day after that she got up, but didn't go to work. I called and talked briefly with her about 8:30 A.M. She was depressed. Then she mowed the lawn, and after that she had a bowl of soup. And after that she went down the hall to her bedroom, locked the door, lay down on the floor, and shot herself in the heart.

INTRODUCTION

What is a suicide survivor? Usually the term "survivors" refers to the relatives listed in obituaries who are left behind after a death, but here suicide survivor means any person who is grieving a suicide death. One can grieve just as deeply for a friend as for a relative. This book is intended to be a guide and support to those of you just starting the awful journey after someone you love has died by suicide.

This book is based on years of study and my own personal experience when my daughter, Lynn, died in 1979. I have also met and known hundreds of other survivors since then. In the word "survivor" there is a challenge to be met: to survive after the most crushing loss that can happen, and to go on. First, however, you need some basic information. (I have written in detail about suicide in my book, *SUICIDE: WHY? — 85 Questions and Answers About Suicide*. AW)

WHAT DOES NOT CAUSE SUICIDE?

Quite a bit of what is "known" about suicide is not so. Suicide is not caused by losing jobs, having fights with people, or having ambitious parents who move a lot.

We can blame anything or anyone for a suicide, but neither will be the *cause* of a suicide. The social conditions we live in affect us and our lives, but neither poverty nor enormous wealth account for suicide. Living in anxious times does not cause suicide; stress and pressure do not cause suicide.

Bad parenting does not cause suicide, and good parenting does not prevent suicide. If it were, then all the children of "bad" parents would kill themselves, but they don't. It also does not account for why children of "good" parents kill themselves. Divorce and broken homes do not cause suicide. Fifty percent of marriages end in divorce these days anyway.

Suicide represents about 1.5 percent of all deaths. There are millions upon millions of people in the population, but only that small fraction kill themselves each year. There has to be something extra that accounts for these deaths.

MYTHS AND FACTS

About forty years ago, someone made a list they called "Myths and Facts About Suicide." Over the years, it has been copied over and over stating several "facts" about suicide that are not so.

Among the so-called "myths" and "facts" are:
• Are people who kill themselves "crazy?" No.
• Are people who kill themselves mentally ill? No.
• Is suicide inherited? No.

These "facts" deny a connection between mental illness and suicide, because both mental illness and suicide are so stigmatized that people dealing with mental illness don't want the additional stigma of being associated with suicide, and people who have suicides in their families don't want the added burden of mental illness.

The people who wrote these "facts" also contend that depression is not an illness; they say that depression is normal and that everyone gets depressed. That is not true. Everyone gets unhappy, sad, blue, regretful, miserable, and all the other shades and varieties of normal human sadness.

Another of these "facts" denies any connection with a genetic inheritance. The fact that these diseases have genetic components is wonderful news. It alerts us that people in our families may be predisposed to these diseases just as others have vulnerabilities to heart disease, alcoholism or diabetes in their families.

The question about "crazy" should ask, "Are people who kill themselves psychotic (out of touch with reality)?" The correct answer is that a few are, but the great majority of people who kill themselves have unrecognized and untreated major depression often concealed by illegal drugs or alcohol. Major depression used to be, and still is by some, called clinical depression.

THE OLD MESSAGE

Most of what is "known" about suicide carries the old message that if suicidal persons are loved and understood well enough, and listened to carefully enough by caring people, and allowed to talk out their problems, they will not kill themselves. This thinking resulted primarily from the belief that suicide stems from unresolved conflicts and psychic injuries that have to be "talked out."

Some people still believe that "depression is anger turned inward," which was an old way of looking at the anger seen in people who have major depression. Now we know that this anger results from the fact that one of the chief symptoms of major depression is irritability. People who live with someone who has major depression often say that they had to "walk on eggshells" to keep from "setting them off."

THE SUICIDE PREVENTION MOVEMENT

About the time the myths and facts were written there also came the "suicide prevention movement." Starting with the fact that often suicidal people are very upset and in crisis, and that they can be "talked down" from their emotional storm, the idea arose of creating a suicide prevention phone line that would be manned by volunteer lay people trained in intervention techniques. The concept took hold, and suicide prevention lines were started all over the country. Why not? They hardly cost anything. The only problem was that they did not prevent suicide.

More properly it should have been called the "suicide *intervention* movement." It became clear that only a very small percentage of calls to these phones involved a suicidal person. Eventually they were called "crisis" or "hotlines" handling a wide variety of problems. They are very effective and helpful in doing this, but after a suicide in a community, there is still a knee jerk reaction to put in a hotline.

SUICIDE IS A BEHAVIOR

Suicide is a behavior. One has actually to commit some action to hurt or kill oneself, and there are degrees of suicidal behavior. Suicidal behavior is on a scale, or continuum, from zero to a hundred with only one hundred as death. Every behavior below one hundred is a frantic, and finally despairing attempt, to find solutions other than death.

These include obvious behavior such as threatening or attempting suicide, reckless driving, or abusing illegal drugs. These are often attempts to find solutions other than death for overwhelming emotional pain.

Most people who write or speak about suicide start with the danger signs, but that is almost too late. The danger signs are about ninety-five on that behavioral scale. To reduce suicide, it is necessary to go back to twenty or twenty-five on the scale when the symptoms of mental illness first show themselves.

CAUSES OF SUICIDE

The causes of suicide actually are multiple, and don't involve dramatic scenes of tragedy or failure in love. The causes have to do with 1) the biology of a person's brain, 2) their genetic inheritance, 3) the psychology of their mind or personality, 4) events in their lives and 5) the society that surrounds them. There are no villains here to blame; a suicidal person has a combination of these factors that put him or her in danger of death.

One researcher calls it "The overlap model for understanding suicidal behavior."[1] This says that suicide results from a *combination* of the biology of the brain, family history and genetics, personality traits, life events or chronic physical illness.

What have been called "mental illnesses" are actually brain diseases, and the brain is just another organ of our body like heart or lungs. The brain has chemicals in it that regulate how we think, how we feel and how we behave. Brain diseases and mental illness will be used interchangeably in this book. Basically, when these chemicals get out of balance in various ways, a person will have 1) major depression, 2) manic-depression, 3) anxiety diseases, or 4) schizophrenia. These are the primary brain diseases from which suicide results.[2–6]

People who have manic-depression and schizophrenia usually have such extreme symptoms that people recognize they are ill. They have psychotic symptoms such as hallucinations and delusions, plus an inability to think and speak normally. Psychotic means being out of touch with reality. Hallucinations cause a person to see and hear things that are not there, and a delusion is a fixed false belief in which, for example, a person believes he is destitute when he, in fact, has $200,000 in a box under his bed.

Schizophrenia affects the ability of people to think and perceive reality. Major depression, manic-depression and anxiety disease primarily affect a person's mood and emotions. They all result from a chemical imbalance in the brain.

The majority of people who kill themselves have major depression. The balance of suicide deaths result from the other three brain diseases. Sometimes they are in combination; anxiety disease is often seen with major depression as is substance abuse. People who have anxiety diseases attempt suicide more often than people who have major depression. [7] One percent of people who attempt suicide will kill themselves within a year, and 10 to 20 percent of people who attempt suicide will ultimately die by suicide. [8]

Evidence reveals that people who kill themselves had a "psychiatric disorder" (brain disease), and that the majority of these suicides resulted from major depression. [9–13] It also reveals "that most people who commit suicide were suffering from a major psychiatric illness at the time of their death, although only a small percentage were being treated." [14–16]

MAJOR DEPRESSION

Major depression is the brain disease from which the majority of suicides result. At any given time, there are about twelve to fifteen million people who have major depression. Eighty percent of them can be successfully treated with medicine, psychotherapy, or in combination of the two, but only 20 percent of people who have depression get any treatment.

The majority of people who have killed themselves had unrecognized, undiagnosed and untreated major depression. Various symptoms of major depression (such as irritability, loss of concentration, poor sleep and an inability to feel pleasure) lead to disruptions in relationships in marriage, work and school.

To the untrained eye these symptoms often look like deliberate and willful angry words and actions — things the depressed person could change or stop if he or she wanted to. Untreated, these symptoms can eventually disrupt and destroy marriages, friendships, school achievements and careers. These end results are the consequences of the depression not the cause of the suicide.

There are some people who receive good medical and psychological treatment who still kill themselves, just as the sickest people with heart disease will also die, even with the best treatment available. The tragedy is that 15 percent of the people who have untreated major depression will ultimately kill themselves. This is the pool from which most suicides result. Most often their families and friends did not know they were sick until they died.

If you are a suicide survivor, you have a long and terrible road ahead of you. I do not want you to have to walk it alone.

ADINA WROBLESKI

September 1991

CHAPTER 1

THE WORST HAS HAPPENED

There is a story about the mother of a family talking to John; she is telling him he must go to school. "But I don't want to," he says. "You must," she replies. He complains, "I don't want to; all the kids pick on me." She says, "Never mind, you have to go to school." He says, "I don't want to; all the teachers pick on me too." "Never mind," she says, "John, you are the principal and you *have* to go to school!"

BECAUSE WE HAVE TO

When devastating grief hits us, we feel much the same way about life. We don't want to go on; we just want to stop. Our emotional pain feels so crippling that we think we can never go on again. We can think neither forward nor backward without pain. The reason we do go on, however, is because *we are the principal in our lives, and we have to go on*. We go on to plant a stake in the future when we feel least able to do it. We go on for our own sake, for our family's, for our friends and for the memory of someone we loved who died.

Suicide! That awful word — that word that has always been whispered when it happened in someone else's family. Suicide! The word that used to make us wonder about "that family" where a suicide occurred.

SUICIDE SURVIVORS

Survivors are the names of the people listed in the obituary — the deceased's living close family or friends. Now, *you* are the survivor of the tragedy — the awful tragedy of suicide death. But you are not alone; you are joined to several million people who are also suicide survivors.

You will meet some of them; some of your friends will suddenly confide that they too had a suicide in their family. But why *confide?* Why not tell? Why didn't you know before? Why should suicide be any worse than cancer or a heart attack?

TABOO AND STIGMA

Almost since the beginning of time, people have tried to "outlaw" suicide by placing a taboo on the subject, and a stigma on the people who killed themselves and on their families. A tabooed subject is something society decides is so terrible that no one may be allowed to do it, talk or learn about it. A stigma is the mark of shame and ridicule placed on those people who do kill themselves, and on their families. The stigma is the punishment for breaking the taboo. There are still some people who shun families who have experienced a suicide.

As badly as you may be feeling as you read this, take some comfort that things are much better now. Society used to do terrible things in the aftermath of suicide. They used to mutilate the bodies of suicides, hang their bodies in town squares, bury their bodies without religious rites and outside the cemetery. They would bury them at a crossroad with a stake driven through their heart. They would confiscate the money of persons who killed themselves, and would drive their families from their homes.

Some of these things still exist. There are still insurance policies that deny life insurance and even hospitalization payments for those who die by suicide.

THE NEW PUNISHMENTS

The families of teenage suicides are punished in new ways. Students at their schools are not permitted to attend their funerals. Schools refuse to allow memorial tree plantings in memory of a student suicide. One family offered a school their memorial moneys for a scholarship in their son's name. The school was willing to accept the scholarship, but refused to put his name on it.

These things are done under the guise of not wanting to make suicide "attractive," " romantic," or "glamorous" to young people. Behind this is the ridiculous belief that suicide is contagious in teenagers. A study published in a prestigious journal, and which received widespread publicity in 1986, claimed that reporting teen suicides or seeing programs about suicides will cause other teens to kill themselves.[1] Four studies, the final one by the Center for Disease Control (CDC), were unable to achieve the same results. [2–4]

The CDC study reported that "We did not demonstrate increased exposure to media presentations of suicide among those who killed themselves. In fact, these teenagers were reported to be less likely to have seen television shows about suicide." [5] The effects of this belief that suicide is contagious is causing horrific punishment on grieving survivors.

The memories of those teens who die by suicide are not allowed to be commemorated. "Experts" — many with impressive degrees, have told the schools that going to the funeral of a suicide should not be allowed. They say it will suggest to his friends that "all the attention paid" to a suicide victim will cause them to say to themselves, "Hey, look at all the attention John is getting at his funeral! Golly, I think I'll go kill myself too." It is as if a teenager would say, "Wow! David hanged himself! Hanging is so glamourous, I think I'll do it too." It is as if another will say, "Gee, all that blood is so romantic! I think I'll shoot myself too."

What is happening is that just when the centuries-old religious taboo has been easing up, we now find some people attempting to re-impose an elitist taboo. Those people say it is all right (safe) for them to talk about suicide, but dangerous for anyone else. And, above all, we must not talk, write, or learn about suicide.

There are still a few churches that deny religious burial to suicides. There are still some denominations that think suicide is a sin. How did a cause of death become a sin? Well, a lot of harm in the world is done by well-meaning people, and around 400 years after the birth of Jesus, well-meaning people thought they could prevent suicide by passing a religious law against it — by making it a sin.

People, then as now, did so because they really thought that suicide was a *choice* that suicidal people voluntarily took. In those days, they knew nothing about the chemicals in a person's brain that affect how they think, feel and behave — the chemicals that can get so out of balance that people kill themselves. They naively thought that if a person saw how much suffering it would cause their family, they would not kill themselves. They were proved tragically wrong.

Suicide continued down through the centuries, as it does today. The difference is that there is unparalleled promise of recovery from a suicidal depression today. The similarity with the past is that too few people today know that depression is a brain disease that can be treated with medicines and psychotherapy, and a disease from which most people could recover. The medicine is needed to correct the chemical imbalance in the brain, and psychotherapy to sort out the problems that result from the depression. Without this knowledge, ancient superstition and modern ignorance combine to keep suicide rates high.

TOO MANY SUICIDES ARE NOT ENOUGH

In addition to the chilling effect the taboo has on research into suicide, the reason there is so little interest in suicide is that *not very many people kill themselves*. Even with suicide being the eighth leading cause of death in the population, and the second leading cause of death among young people, there are not enough suicides to get more than momentary attention from people who don't want to see it at all.

For example, in the United States, every year 5,000 young people (ages fifteen through twenty-four) kill themselves, but the population of young people is 20 million. That isn't enough to make people care. Out of a population of 240 million people, 30,000 kill themselves every year. Apparently 30,000 suicides aren't enough to make people really care.

In the mid-1980s, the public heard many voices
saying that teenage suicide had reached "epidemic"
proportions. Parents were scared and concerned for their
children. But fear lasts only so long. Since millions and
millions of parents' children didn't kill themselves, their
heightened fear subsided. The public felt deceived by
people who tried to whip up concern about teenage suicide
when they looked around and saw that their children
weren't killing themselves.

It also sent a message to the public that only teenage
suicides mattered, and this was tragically unfair. No one
had told them the truth: that teenage suicide is rare. Few
young people die of anything. Sociologist, Ronald Maris,
had the courage to say that "one question no one...has
asked about young people is why so *few* of them suicide."
[6] Teenagers represent about 7 percent of all suicides. If
the hue and cry had been about *all* suicides, enough people
might have been mobilized to demand more attention be
paid to suicide. It wasn't that people said to themselves,
"I'm not going to care about teenage suicide," but that they
didn't like being scared and fooled.

SUICIDE IN YOUR FAMILY

But when suicide occurs in *your* family or to your
friend, it is not rare; it is a gigantic fact of life. When it is
your husband, wife, child, brother, sister, mother, father or
friend, it is *your* whole world that is torn apart.

There are so many survivors. For every suicide,
there are at least ten people closely affected by the death.
That means that for the 33,500 suicides each year, (30,000
in the United States and 3,500 in Canada) there are at least
335,000 people who become new suicide survivors. In just

ten years, that means another three million new suicide survivors.

The general public has been so bombarded by confusing and misleading messages, it has not realized it needs to energize itself with righteous indignation. The public needs to tell the experts that if they don't have answers, they had better learn them. The public needs to demand this, and suicide survivors need to lead the way. If suicide survivors ever become organized, they can demand that priority be given to preventing suicide. They have the numbers to get things done.

It is a tragic fact that we have the tools right now to prevent thousands of suicides every year, and they are not being widely used. With the present arsenal of medicines and psychotherapies now available to treat depression, we could substantially reduce the number of suicides every year. It will be the same as was the case with diabetes deaths when insulin was discovered. There must be a commitment to see that these tools are used on the part of the government, medical, psychological and sociological communities, as well as business, the media and the public. Until there is such commitment we are saying by our inaction, "We really don't care."

SOMEONE YOU LOVE HAS DIED

But who cares? Right now you are dealing with the fact of suicide, not its history or social implications. Someone *you* loved has died. This makes everything different. It is often imagined that the death of a child is the worst thing that can happen to a person, and when it is the suicide death of *your* child, it is the "worst" — whether he or she was fifteen or fifty years old. Almost all the publicity about suicide concerns young people who die, however, and this minimizes and ignores the grief of many thousands of people every year.

It is a tragic fact that about that 5,000 elderly people kill themselves each year. But we don't value our wonderful old people as we should. One cynic said, "An old lady takes an overdose of her medicine. She's old and she's dead; who cares how she died?" (There are even people who say we should "help" old people kill themselves — the so-called "rational suicide" advocates.) These older people who kill themselves have spouses and children and grandchildren and friends who grieve. They matter too — those who die, and those who survive them.

Then there are all the people who kill themselves who are not very old or very young. They are the men and women in their late twenties to early sixties. All these people too, have parents, spouses, children, brothers and sisters, other relatives and friends. These people matter too — those who die, and those who survive them.

Parents, spouses, children, brothers and sisters — these are the primary people that matter — those most affected by all suicide deaths. But suicide causes pain to other relatives and friends. It causes pain and shock among acquaintances. So when is suicide the worst? It is the worst when someone *you* love has died.

THE WORST HAS HAPPENED

Suicide! It has happened in your family or to your friend. You feel stunned; you feel the worst shock you have ever received. It seems like the suicide death came suddenly and from nowhere. You have a funeral to plan, or to go to. Your feeling of shock is real; it is your body's protective response to terrible pain.

Grief is like a raging river, and shock is like ice on that river that enables one to walk on it — to do the things we have to do. But the ice is thin in places and we fall through, and have to climb out again, and go on. Eventually, through the many months ahead, that river of grief will gradually change to a brook and finally to a small stream.

But that is months and months away. Shock continues to be your friend. It helps you get through the funeral, going back to work and your daily routine, and finally leaves when you are once again strong enough to walk alone. Why say months and months instead of years and years? Because there are too many dire and pessimistic forecasts about suicide grief. You will hear people say:

- that your guilt will be massive and overwhelming;
- that you were somehow in complicity in the death;
- that you will not be able to "admit" it was a suicide;
- that your marriage will probably breakup;
- that if only you had loved and understood well enough or listened well enough, the suicide would have been prevented;
- that you and your family are now at high risk for suicide;
- that you will be "arrested in your grief" and need intensive therapy; and
- that you will never "get over" a suicide death — that you will (should) suffer from it all your life.

You may hear some or all of these things, and you may think or fear some or all of them will be true. It may *seem* they are all true, but given your experience, these are normal thoughts and fears. In the pain of grief, however, you may be particularly vulnerable to self-fulfilling prophecies. You will have a terrible scar, and it will pain you from time to time for the rest of your life.

It is never going to get worse than it is now. Hang on to that thought. There are many dark days and months of grief ahead, but remember that you got through the worst; you will get through the rest. You will go back and forth — believing and not believing that someone you loved has died. You will suffer, and suffering is painful! But on your dark days *remember that the worst that can happen already has.*

Suicide survivors have a right to recovery from their grief as other people do. You will survive — because people have always survived — because they had to. It is what makes us human — that we go on and become stronger and better because of the pain in our lives. You are the principal in your school of life and you *have* to go on.

LIVING WHILE GRIEVING

But first you must grieve while going on. No one has ever been immune to suffering. The pain of your grief may hit you right away, or shock may stay a month or so, and then plunge you into that raging river of grief. Whether the pain hits you early or is delayed, it will feel like you are drowning in it, and you will feel convinced it will never go away. *Feel that. Give into the pain when you can.* Cry, if that is the way you grieve. Beat your fists on the wall, go to the grave and scream at him or her, or just sit tight and endure if that is the way you grieve. Don't let any one tell you *how* to grieve.

We have a feminine, middle class standard of what proper grief is. Traditionally, men have not grieved by crying, or crying a lot, as women do. It has been fashionable to fault men for this, and it is good that young men are increasingly learning that they can be vulnerable and cry. But the only way a lot of men in our society *can grieve* is by "toughing it out" — by "holding it all in." We must recognize the difference in the way men and women grieve in our society, and not blame men for being what they are.

There was a tradition in our now changing society that told men they *had to* "pull themselves together." The presumption was that women, being more sensitive, needed more time to grieve. The presumption was that women grieved *more* than men.

But people flow into vacuums. In the past, if men were told they must return to work immediately, they did it because they had to. If women were permitted more time, it is human that they took it, and it is human that they flowed into the roles that society cast for them. With more equality between the sexes, we are seeing changes — women are treated as men in the work force, and they are behaving as men have: "toughing things out" at work and "pulling themselves together" at home for the family's sake *because they have to.*

Our country was founded by men and women at a time when it was the norm to lose two or three children to death; and our pioneer women may not have worked outside the home, but they worked side by side with men "toughing things out" and making things work. People grieve as they always have; we grieve at the same time as we continue living and moving toward the future.

It will not be easy, but whoever said, or expected, suffering to be easy? What kind of a person would you be if you could quickly "get over" the death of someone you loved so deeply? You have a long period of grief ahead of you; you will be changed by it; your life will be forever changed by it.

There is a saying that when you lose a parent, you lose your past; that when you lose your child you lose the future. That is not true. You cannot lose your past; your past cannot be changed. You cannot lose your future; your future is continuously being changed into the present. It is up to you how you live in the future, and it is up to you how you react to events in the present. It will be hard to go back to life, but you will.

WHAT WILL HAPPEN?

It is never too late to grieve. The suicide death you are grieving may have happened a week, several months or years ago. The reason it is necessary to grieve — to feel all the pain and all the emotions associated with grief — is to help us rebuild our lives without the person we loved so much.

Whether it was your child, spouse, parent, grandparent, sibling, or friend who died, there is now a huge, gaping hole in your life where all your memories of the past and dreams for the future combined to make your life meaningful with someone you loved who died.

What's ahead? Lots of pain, anxiety and heartbreak. Each day may seem like it is worse than the other, but each day you endure your grief will be a building block of your future. It is hard to realize this day by day, so it is best if you do just that: go from day to day.

An important part of grieving is to check on yourself. At first it is just enough to get through one day. Many grieving people are surprised when they look back after two months, for example, to find they *are* a bit better. Not much, but a bit better. The period of time is past when they thought they couldn't make it through, and they're still holding on and going forward.

People are very impatient in grief — they want it to "be over," and quickly. We are not as realistic about emotional pain as we are about physical pain. If we break a bone, we *expect* it to be painful, maybe agonizingly painful, but we remind ourselves that it will get better.

Our experience with pain tells us this, but we seem to forget it when our pain is emotional. If your spouse, or parent,or brother, or sister, or child, or friend has died, you cannot "get over it" quickly. If you could, it would mean there was not very much love there in the first place.

It is helpful to look back and compare, and to measure your progression through grief. You will discover that grief is one of the most chaotic experiences you will ever have. Some people also think that your *first grief* may be the worst, because you do not have the experience to call on as we do in physical pain. We grieve differently for different people, and in accordance to our relationship with them.

BACK TO A NEW NORMAL

Things will never be back to the *"old normal;"*
grief means building a *"new normal."* People tend to take
things for granted, but death is no respecter of times or
occasions. Our grief after a loved one's death interrupts our
lives; it seems to cut us off at the knees. It feels as if the
bottom has dropped out of our world.

Who will be your guide? You need to call on all the
resources in your life for support: your spirituality, your
family, your organizations, your work, your entertainment
and your friends. Learning to grieve may be learning to
share your grief. This is important for families. If everyone
goes around "holding themselves together" it may look as
if no one cares.

You can become a better person, more sensitive to
hurt, and stronger than you were before. You will find a
"new normal" because you *have* to go on living just like the
principal who has to go to school.

CHAPTER 2

DEALING WITH OTHER PEOPLE

After the death of someone you love, every day may seem an ordeal, and everything you do may seem extremely difficult. One of those difficulties is that there is so little understanding about suicide death that people often do not know what to say or do in its aftermath. Most people are well-intentioned, but even the best of people may feel inadequate in the face of your pain. They don't know what to say, and sometimes they say things that hurt.

It is not uncommon for people to feel so uncomfortable about suicide that they say nothing for fear of saying the wrong thing, or worse, for them, is that you will cry (so what if you do?). This causes some people to act as if nothing has happened, which is pretty extraordinary in the face of a suicide death. Some people may fail to talk about the person who died; they may act as if he or she never died. It's hard to keep perspective, but most people intend well; they just may not always know how to act that way. You do not have to go out of your way to help them help you, however.

Another thing to remember is that this is a time of super- sensitivity on your part; six weeks or six months after your tragedy, acquaintances may well forget, or not realize that you are still deeply in pain. It may seem as if your world has stopped, and everyone else is speeding by you.

Remember the wisdom of the musical title: "Stop the World, I Want To Get Off." Your world has stopped, and it will be a while before you get back up and on with your life again. At first, you will just take short trips out into the world again, but eventually your life will get back on the road of your future.

TRYING TO UNDERSTAND

Some people say you will *never* know *why* someone you loved killed him or herself. Well, that is true and untrue. This whole book is about trying to help you understand why the suicide happened from a medical and psychological point of view — to give you factual information about suicide and why people die by it.

The *why* you will never know is that haunting question: What was in their mind at the moment they decided the time is "Now?" What were they thinking of? Were they thinking of us? Why didn't they give us another chance? Why didn't they let us know how bad things were? Even those few who were left notes didn't get adequate reasons for their suicide.

More time has been spent blaming people for suicide than finding explanations for suicide. Numerous studies have been made counting the divorces, moves to new communities, ambitious or absent fathers, and smothering mothers in the families of suicides. The assumption is that a lack of love and understanding of the suicidal person was at fault in our relationships — that we didn't love them well enough, pay enough attention to them, and were so preoccupied with our own lives, we ignored their cries for help.

LOVE — UNDERSTANDING — LISTENING

There is a widespread belief that if one just loves and understands people well enough, they will not kill themselves. It is also widely believed that all a suicidal person needs is to be listened to. North Americans have such a touching belief in *talking things out*. Consequently, when people — especially teenagers — do kill themselves, the assumption is that had they been listened to well enough, and loved and understood well enough, by good people, their suicides could, or should, have been prevented.

Conjectures are also made about the sibling rank order in families; overbearing and aggressive mothers and weak fathers are blamed; and speculations are made about childhood losses. Extremely pessimistic predictions are made of the ability to continue without immediate and extensive "counseling" — often involving the whole "sick" family. The fact is, in most suicides someone in the family *was very sick, and they died;* the rest are well.

Think about this. If your parenting was so terrible, why haven't all your children killed themselves? If you were such a terrible wife and person, why was it just your husband who killed himself? If you were such a bad child, why did only one of your parents kill themself? The answer is because someone in your family was very sick, and they died.

Trying to make sense of so shocking and tragic a death as suicide, in the face of your own and society's blame, is more than one person should have to bear. You feel you can't carry on, but you do. You think it is more than you can bear, but it isn't. You feel it is tragically unfair, and it is. You feel you will never get over this, but

you will. Why? *Because you have to* — just as all those
millions of suicide survivors since the beginning of people
on earth did before you — in the face of even worse
censure and punishment than we have now.

Will you always have a scar? Of course. Will it hurt
from time to time in the future? Of course. Will you feel
better and eventually get back on the road of life? Yes.
Ultimately, it is not *how* they died, but *that* they died that is
so terrible.

HOW MUCH, AND HOW LONG WILL IT HURT?

The pain and shock of grief soon after a death hurts
so much that many people want to know how long it will be
before they are "over it." You think it is too much to bear.
Too many people say a suicide death is something you will
never get over, and there is an the implication that you
shouldn't get over it. Some slightly more cheerful people
will tell you that — *if* you do get over it — it will take
years. Sometimes that is true of a few people, but most
people survive, endure, return to the future, and are happy
again. That doesn't mean it will be easy. No one ever
promised a rose garden in life, and no one ever said
suffering is easy, but throughout history people have
suffered, been changed, and become better and happy
again.

The work of grief is to linger and say good-bye to
the one you loved, and eventually take those intense
feelings and once again apply them to the present and
future. You do not ever want to forget someone you loved
who died, but it is in the nature of humans to forget pain.
It's hard to believe at first, but it will happen — the pain

gets less and goes away. You will remember it from time to time, and feel pain, but that is not the same as "never getting over it." To make the suicide death of someone you loved the focal point of your life is not fair to yourself, your family, or friends.

For centuries society has recognized the collective experience of humans that grief takes a year or two to resolve. Going through grief, however, is like climbing up a mountain that has a lot of peaks and valleys; there are ups and downs, but movement is upwards. Grief is a huge emotional wound, and it takes time to heal. But time, by itself, will not help you get "over it." If you just stay still, holding all your pain inside, it will lie waiting for you. The more you stamp down your pain, the more it will hurt. Time needs some help from you. You need to grieve in your own way, and you need to go on. While all the turmoil and pain is happening to you, you *have* to do your work, you *have* to care for and about the rest of your family (if you are alone, your responsibility and care are for yourself) and you *have* to be with, and care about other people outside your family.

Is there any agenda for grief? Yes and no. People vary. Usually, however, the first two months are the worst; they are when you feel most hopeless. Some people feel relatively numb the first month, and then the pain hits; other people feel absolute despair right away, hardly thinking they can pull themselves together. After a couple of months, there is enough time to look back — often in amazement — and realize you did get through "all that." And it is good to compare; remember how you felt at the funeral, for example, and gauge what you have accomplished since then. Aren't you just a little bit better? It may only be that you got from there to here, but that's progress. About three months after the suicide, you start to concentrate better, and it`s a little easier to fall asleep. You may still cry a lot, but not as much as you did before. It still seems a pretty bumpy road you are trudging along.

Through all this misery, suddenly it's six months since someone you loved died. You wonder how you ever made it this far. But what a terrible thing it seems that the world is impersonal and goes on heedless of your pain. You can "get off the world" for awhile during grief, but the world still goes round and round, so you can get back on again. You are the principal in your life, and you have to go back to living. It is this process of *having to go on* — at the same time as you are grieving — that makes grief normal, and you stronger.

THE HURT AND PAIN OF RECOVERY

Feeling guilty for feeling happy is called *recovery guilt*. Perhaps you saw a movie or had lunch with a friend — and you enjoyed it! You suddenly realize you have gone two whole hours without thinking of someone you loved who died. You *knew* you would never forget; you *vowed* you would never forget. And here you did; you had a good time, and you feel guilty about it. It may not seem like it, but this is progress — this is good news for you. Recovery guilt can happen anytime. It did, perhaps, after the funeral when everyone got together, and there were old friends and distant relatives, and you laughed and talked with them. Many people wonder how they could forget at a time like that. They "forget" because that's our mind's way of giving us a little break, and giving us the first indication that we are going to be all right — the fact that we can still laugh is our first hopeful indication.

It is not uncommon, about six to eight months after the death, to have a big setback. Maybe it's prompted by recovery guilt; maybe it's a reluctance to begin to let the past start to slip away. Whatever its cause, to you it feels as if you are right back at the beginning. It feels as if all the progress you thought you'd made is gone, and you were wrong to think you would ever be better. But it *is* a setback. Maybe it is a stop to rest before you set off to climb the rest of the way back onto the world and into the future.

Somewhere around the midpoint in your grief, the pain begins to feel less sharp — to feel as if it's a dull ache that you will live with forever. You won't. Most people who talk about grief forget to remind you that *people forget pain*. You have to call on your experience to remember this — to believe that even the horror of a suicide death will diminish. But first you need to give yourself a chance. If one drew a line to represent the months after grief, it would be very jagged, but the overall course would be steadily upward. What happens is that as you get further from the death, the times you are down begin to get less deep, and the times between your low points begin to be further apart. As you approach the one-year anniversary, you feel pretty good most of the time, and the sharp pain and dull ache changes to a heavy sadness.

You need to be aware that grieving people may also have major depression. Over a period of months, if the intensity of your pain is not relieved, if you lose weight, sleep poorly, and feel desperate and hopeless, you should see your doctor. Since 4 out of 100 people get depression, and since it is already in your family, it is wise to watch for it in yourself and others in your family.

GETTING "OVER IT"

You will think, and hear "experts" tell you that you will *never* get over a suicide death — especially if it is one of your children. If getting "over it" means being happy and productive again, yes you will. If getting "over it" means forgetting the death and all that has happened, you won't. The holidays or their birthday may always bring back painful memories, but it will change to having a good cry two or three years afterwards, and a short period of sadness many years after the death.

One of the difficult things for you at first will be going to other funerals. You may always cry a little in remembrance, but what makes you human is that you care. Other things that are difficult are seeing other couples together if it was your spouse who died, or seeing mothers or fathers and their children together if your child died, or just seeing other people having a good time. You may get angry at them for appearing so happy, and for appearing to take each other for granted. You vow this will never happen to you again, and keeping that vow is one of the good things that can come out of grief.

WOMEN, GUILT AND GRIEF

Clear genetic, biological, psychological and sociological links are present in brain diseases and suicide. Despite all these factors governing each human, mothers and women generally have been held responsible for the psychological health of the entire family. Folk wisdom says, "The hand that rocks the cradle, rules the world," and "Behind every good man there is a good woman." The actual power of women has always been a good deal less;

the placing of responsibility, blame and guilt has always been a great deal more.

Two researchers studied major psychiatric and psychological clinical journals for the incidence of mother-blaming. They wanted to know if the women's movement during the 1970s had affected the amount of mother-blaming involved in the psychological health of families. It hadn't. "Professional ideology...crystallized by the 1950s, in which the causation of all psychopathology, from simple behavior problems to juvenile delinquency to schizophrenia itself, was laid at the doorstep of the mother. The guilt and anxiety created in mothers whose children had even minor behavior deviations were enormous."

In the same study researchers repeated the traditional notion that "women's physiology and hormones — but not men's — naturally suit them for child rearing. What has not been pointed out is that, if women come by child-rearing skills naturally, it is curious that they (are blamed for) emotional disturbances in so many of their children." They also said, "mothers were by far the most likely to be discussed" and the "authors of the 125 articles read for this study attributed to mothers a total of 72 different kinds of psychopathology" in their children. "In no article was the mother's relationship with the child described as simply healthy, nor was she ever described only in positive terms." [1]

What does this have to do with suicide and grief? Well, if women are considered to be more responsible for how their children turn out, they are then more likely to feel guilty and are thought to grieve more. Historically, as today, women are thought to grieve more deeply than men. They are *expected* to grieve more, and they often are treated differently from men after a suicide. People expect men to tough things out and be strong for the sake of the women and children, and women are expected to *feel* more deeply. Women often are given more time off after a suicide death — especially the death of a child. It is assumed they *need* more time to "pull themselves together" than men. Men had no choice; their role was to be the strong supporter.

Now that women are seeking and approaching equality, these assumptions of weakness and the need for more time to recover are still being held by society, but many more women now are in the same position as men. Most working women have no more choice now than men do as employees; they are given three days off for the funeral and expected back at work. Many women now say that they wanted to go right back to work because it helped them keep their mind off their pain. But the point of this discussion is not to say that old or new assumptions are good or bad, but to point out that when the same expectations are made for women as for men, they perform the same — *because they have to*.

ROCK MUSIC AND SATANISM

Other kinds of blaming are certainly alive. Some of the new targets are the ever unpopular rock music and Satanism. There have been a few lawsuits and many claims that certain rock bands cause some teenage suicides. In one famous case, two teenage suicides were blamed on the English rock group Judas Priest. The parents sued the group, but the judge ruled that claimed subliminal messages urging teens to "do it" were chance sounds in no way related to the deaths. In an article blaming the parents of the boys, a writer claimed the lawsuit was a "sad attempt by grieving grown-ups to find blame for their own failures." [2]

As for Satanism, adults have made this another hot button for some teens to push. Even though a few teens who kill themselves may have dabbled in Satanism, a far larger group of teenagers who killed themselves went to church, but we do not blame religion for their suicides. A small number of teens who played Dungeons and Dragons killed themselves, but a far larger number played Nintendo games. Society always has an eye out for unpopular causes for which to blame suicide. When these are absent society can go back to the old faithful mother-blaming.

RELIGION AND GRIEF

The fact that *you have to go on* is the hope of the future. The worst of all things about grief is the temporary loss of hope. It is rebuilding hope that is the work of grief. You may think you can't do this now, and perhaps, right now, you can't. But know that you will.

Most people today have grown up with a legacy of fear and shame about suicide. Before there was scientific understanding of suicide, it seemed to people that suicide was something people did deliberately — sometimes to hurt other people. Hundreds of years ago in our culture, people thought that they could prevent suicide by making it a sin. It was a vain attempt, and it caused centuries of pain for suicide survivors. There are still some churches that preach that the soul of a suicide will suffer eternal damnation, but they are very few. Some people are surprised to find that it has been many years since the Catholic Church had harsh and punitive attitudes toward suicide. Today the religious community is in the forefront of concern for genuine suicide prevention, and for the care of survivors when prevention fails.

The death of someone we love shakes our faith in ourselves. The work of grief is also rebuilding our faith — in ourselves, and daring to place it again in others. Hope and faith are two of the most important religious principles there are, and that is why so many people find that their religion plays so large a part in being a fortress against despair.

You may feel supported by your religion, or temporarily betrayed. Many people feel that doubt is an important part of religion. Your religion may be of any faith — Protestant, Catholic, Jewish, Muslim, Humanist or any of the number of other ways people relate to their spirituality. Spirituality is the part of us that helps us transcend or rise above ourselves — the part that makes us better and stronger. Most people will find their churches and synagogues very supportive, and their pastors, priests and rabbis willing and able to help.

CHAPTER 3

WHY IS THIS GRIEF SO DIFFERENT?

Research on suicide grief has found that suicide survivors have extra problems due to the taboo and stigma, but despite this, recover as other people do. [1–6] A case could be made that suicide survivors are sturdier than other grieving people because they recover despite all the extra problems they have.

BEWILDERMENT

"We did not know, and the professionals we dealt with did not know she was sick until she died!" "We never knew anything was wrong until he died." Only in suicide death are survivors put in this ludicrous position. The taboo and stigma have prevented public education about suicide. There has been virtually no public education about depression, and what little education there has been about depression and suicide sometimes has been confusing and many times, outright wrong. They say, "We did not know he had problems (not a disease) until he died." It is little wonder that you may be feeling that your loved one was a perfectly healthy person one minute, and the next minute dead by his or her own hand? It is no wonder you are left feeling there were no clues, and that the death mysteriously came "out of the blue?"

It is popular to say that "Why?" is the one question that will never be answered about suicide death. It's interesting that people don't use the words "never", "ever", and "forever" about other causes of death. We are much more realistic and optimistic about other deaths. It is almost as if the taboo and stigma say we *should* never be allowed the gradual recovery that occurs in other deaths — that we *should* be left in the dark about our loved one's death.

There are two aspects of the question "Why?" The first we can know; that is, "Why did they die?" The simple, but truthful, answer is that the person we loved so much got so sick (usually with depression) that they died, and the way someone dies from depression is by suicide. The chemicals in their brains that affected how they thought, felt and behaved were out of balance, causing them to view the future and their world as places they could no longer live — places where it was too painful to live.

The "why?" that we won't know is why they decided that, after all the pain they`d been through — after all the things they had tried to make their pain go away — after all that others had tried to do for them — *"now"* was the time for them to die. On the day that my daughter killed herself, what made her decision after lunch that *"now"* was the time when absolutely all hope was gone? That is the "why?" I will never know.

DENIAL OF THE CAUSE OF DEATH

It used to be more common to "cover up" a suicide death than it is today, but it still occurs. The oppressive stigma makes some people feel they will help themselves, and protect the good name of the person who died by saying it was an accident or a heart attack — anything but a suicide.

Nonetheless, it is still fairly common to lie in some circumstances and to some people about the cause of death; for example, a family may tell the truth to everyone but eighty-year-old Grandma who lives a thousand miles away. They think it is "nicer" for her not to know. They may tell a casual acquaintance the death was a heart attack; it seems simpler to do than dealing with that person's shocked reaction.

Another reason for lying about the cause of death is to avoid the cruel penalties imposed by some insurance policies. Most whole life policies contain "suicide clauses." It is understandable that insurance companies want to protect themselves from the person who kills him or herself and wants the survivors protected by insurance. The irony is that this post-death wish for survivor benefits is granted for people who kill themselves two years *after* the issuance of the policy, but not before. However, few people who kill themselves are thinking of their insurance coverage. If they had been thinking this well, and had logically seen the consequences, they might not have had to kill themselves.

Even worse are some hospitalization policies that will not pay the hospital bills for persons who die by suicide. Not all persons who die by suicide die quickly. Sometimes they are hospitalized from a few to several days. For families to suddenly discover that their hospitalization policies have suicide clauses is devastating. While they are still trying to absorb the fact of the death, they have the additional shock of incurring a huge financial obligation as well.

It is not that insurance companies are unable to foresee and regulate premiums accordingly. Many group life policies do not have suicide clauses, but most individual policies do. If insurance actuaries can compute premiums for all other deaths, they can surely do so for suicide death. Because they don't, some people *have* to lie about the death — just to survive financially. Just the fact that some insurance policies pay off and others don't is a grave injustice. Suicide survivors have not been strong enough so far to band together to demand that they be treated fairly.

In the past, professional people such as doctors, police officers, medical examiners, funeral directors and others often counseled people to cover up the suicide, and "helped" by putting another cause of death on reports. This is not done very often today, because professionals know that it is harmful for families to live the lie of a secret suicide in the family. Caregivers would have never had to "help" people lie if there hadn't been such severe social and financial consequences following from suicide.

Realistically, suicide survivors have to make decisions about what and how much to tell people. A rule of thumb is that it's on a "need to know" basis. If, for example, your child died, and you visit with someone at a coffee counter you will likely never see again, and they ask how many children you have, tell the actual number without elaboration. However, if that person becomes your friend later, he or she needs to know about this major and tragic part of your life.

It is absolutely the best policy, however, to tell the truth about the suicide. It is best for you; it is too difficult to keep juggling lies, and to remember who knows the truth and who doesn't. If other people can't handle the truth, that is their problem. Also if you lie, it suggests that you really are a "bad" person, and have something terrible to hide. You need to marshal all your resources to remember that you and your family are good people who have had a terrible tragedy happen.

THE METHOD OF DEATH

Today most people die away from their homes — usually in hospitals, and most people die nonviolent deaths. But this usually is not true of people who kill themselves. Because people who kill themselves are otherwise physically healthy, they have to resort to shocking and often violent methods of death. And they most often die at home.

A suicide survivor may have the burden of discovering the body, and seeing the death scene of someone who died from gunshot, hanging, carbon monoxide poisoning, or worse. Many survivors have to clean up the death scene of a loved one. Few can afford the luxury of moving, so they must become desensitized to the room where the death occurred. A person whose relative or friend jumped in a river faces the probability of a disfigured body, or the possibility that the body will not be found at all.

Most people who kill themselves do so with methods that are *available* to them, and consequently, most Americans kill themselves with guns. In Canada, where handguns are much less accessible, most people who kill themselves use poisons and hanging. Suicide methods are also culturally determined. In a study of three generations of Chinese male suicides in the United States, a researcher found that the grandfather generation, who had come from China where hanging was the preferred method, continued that method after they came to the United States. Their grandchildren who killed themselves were products of the American culture, however, and used guns.

The more bizarre the suicide method is, the more difficult it is for us to understand. Shocking as suicide death is, it is even more so when people burn themselves to death or barricade themselves with hostages and eventually shoot themselves. It is even harder still to understand homicide-suicide. It is not known why, but there is a chemical in the brain called serotonin, and when one of its component parts is low, it is associated with more violent and aggressive methods.

Some of these people are psychotic (not in touch with reality). A mother who jumps to her death with her child may actually believe she is protecting her baby. But most people who kill themselves are too much in touch with reality — the reality of their desperate, never-ending emotional pain. Their thinking is distorted by the pain.

Some people consciously wish to disguise their suicides, and die in "accidents" of their own making. It also has been widely reported that many single driver car accidents are really suicides. In two studies of single car-single person accidents, it was found that between 2 percent and 5 percent were actually suicides. (There were no attempts to swerve or take protective action before the crash.) Whatever the cause, from the survivor's point of view, dealing with the method of suicide is a problem no other survivors have to contend with.

SEPARATION IN AND OUT OF THE FAMILY

Only in suicide is the first question, "What will we tell people?" Sometimes not every one in the family will be told the truth. This is usually done to "spare them." Only in suicide are there divisions among family and friends that stem from the taboo and stigma.

One of the "comforts" of grief is to blame someone for the death, and nowhere is this easier to do than in suicide. We have been taught to blame. Historically, the stigma placed on the "bad" family suggests blame *should* be placed. While there is not always a scapegoat, spouses, for example, are frequently blamed by in-laws.

Americans have eagerly adopted Freud's belief that all psychological problems originate in childhood, and that to relieve them one has to "talk them out" and "deal with them" or dire consequences will occur. With these ideas came the indictment of suicide survivors that assumed that *if the victims had been loved well enough*, and *listened to well enough* by *good* people, they would not have killed themselves. To this day, these are themes of movies and plays where characters die by suicide. Parents and spouses are usually the people who are blamed; it is assumed that if they had been caring enough, they could have prevented the suicide.

This assumption, along with real grievances within families and among friends, leads to disagreement and separation. As a rule, only in suicide do people find they can talk about the death with some, but not other family members. Only in suicide, do people decide who outside the family they will talk to about the death. The question always is, "Who shall we tell (the truth to)?" Society has taught even the kindliest people to recoil when they hear the word suicide.

RECONSTRUCTION

When people talk about grief they often mention "acceptance." Acceptance is that sought-after goal when we are "over" the pain. In suicide death, acceptance is more difficult because of the bewilderment felt about the cause of death. Sometimes early, sometimes later, we almost always remember things that scared or troubled us when our loved ones were alive — that now seem to make so much sense. They had, for example, talked about suicide, and we pooh-poohed it, or thought they weren't serious. We remember all the many things we could or should have done. We remember all the times when we could have acted better or done more than we did.

Among all the blaming it is perhaps most potent when we blame ourselves, especially if the suicide occurred after harsh words or a parent's punishment of a teen. It also is very common after the breakup of a relationship. Survivors need to remember all the times harsh words were exchanged when the person did not kill him or herself, or how many times a teen had been grounded after which he or she did not kill themself. If breakups of relationships were a cause of suicide, there might be no one left on earth.

It's painful to look back. We see clues that seem so obvious now, but which frightened us at the time — frightened us so much that we "forgot" we heard and saw what now seems so clear. Possibly we remember how difficult it was to live with the one who died. Because he or she wrestled death from nature's hands, and left us no defenses, we alternate our wonder with anger and bitterness. "Why didn't our loved one give us a second chance?" we ask over and over. At a certain point, we have to remember things as they were, rather than the way we bitterly wish they were.

We are so forcefully faced with the way things *are now* that we must begin to remember things *as they were*. Very few people who die are saints, and our people who died often were more difficult to live with than some others. Sometimes suicidal people are angry people, who are difficult to please. Sometimes just seeing their desperate suffering was the worst part of living with them. Sometimes they were so quiet and well-behaved, their death was the loudest thing they ever said.

Whatever your past with someone you loved, you must now build the future without that person. It seems impossible to pull yourself from the past, which is the only place your loved one still lives. But part of suicide grief is to reconstruct the past, without assigning yourself the role of villain. The hard task of grief is to begin to pull yourself back to the present from the past where everything seems so clear now. Reconstruction and acceptance mean we put the past in better perspective. We have to remember the past accurately — that many times we walked the extra mile — that *we did the best we could with what we knew at the time*.

CHAPTER 4

THE MANY PAINS
OF GRIEF

Right now there is the pain! At first it seems it is all one huge pain, but we quickly discover this huge pain is made up of many different kinds. The pains of suicide grief include all the extra problems you have because of the taboo and stigma. On top of that, many common grief reactions have unique characteristics when it is suicide grief.

FEARS

Fear is generally viewed as weakness in our society, so most people suffer with their fears silently. But fear and all the other emotions are what make us human. It is normal and human at this terrible time to have thoughts about our own deaths — even our own suicide deaths. Here you are devastated that someone you love has killed themself; how can you have these awful *thoughts of suicide* popping into your head? You can because it is normal.

Experience has shown that in the aftermath of suicide death, it is not unusual for survivors to have thoughts of suicide. It may sound unusual, but having any kind of awful and terrible thoughts is a symptom of anxiety. If you have occasional sudden, awful, and frightening thoughts of suicide, they are probably symptoms of your anxiety and are normal. If they persist over a long period, and involve specific plans for death, you need to run, not walk to your doctor.

Speaking of your doctor, it is a good idea after the death to have a physical exam. Grief has many physical manifestations — headaches, stomachaches, sleeplessness and poor concentration — and it is reassuring to know that you are healthy, or at least no worse than you were before. Some conditions, such as high blood pressure, may be aggravated by the death, and your doctor may want to give you medication, or watch you more closely for a while.

Because a vulnerability to major depression runs in families, some people get depression while they grieve. Antidepressant medicines are necessary to take away the severe symptoms they may think are reactions to grief. The difference between depression and grief is in the intensity of feelings or reactions. You have reason to suspect depression if there is weight loss over a few months, sleeping is particularly disordered, and the emotional pain is excessively sensitive. Almost all grieving people can give themselves some relief from grief; they can laugh at a joke or be diverted by a movie. People who have depression cannot do this. Check your reactions against the list of symptoms of depression in the back of this book. If four or more symptoms last more than two weeks, see your doctor. It may be that depression is making your grief worse.

Do not fall into the foolishness of thinking medicine is something to be avoided. Some people take pride in "handling things" by themselves without the "crutch" of medication. Medicines are a blessing we are lucky to have; there is no nobility in needless suffering. (What is absolute foolishness is any attempt to "treat" your pain with alcohol or illegal drugs. It may seem to dull your pain, but it does so at great potential harm to you.)

Another very common fear is that *someone else you love will die*. When a spouse dies, the remaining spouse may be more worried about a child or children. Children may be afraid that if one parent died, so could the other. Who you worry about depends on your relationships. But be assured is it normal to have this panicky fear that someone else will die, and what will you do then? With time it will gradually go away with your other fears.

It is also normal in the aftermath of suicide to *worry about mental illness* — even in people who deny a connection between the two. You may wonder who will be struck next. It might be sensible to do so, because illnesses run in families. This may be your first indication that your family has a vulnerability to depression. You need to realize, however, that your family is in no way "foredoomed" because there has been a suicide.

Our health is determined, like our eye color, by the combination of genes we inherit from our parents. Unless we are identical twins, we all inherit different combinations. Even identical twins are not identical in their illnesses or deaths. This is because our destinies are strongly, but only partially determined by our inheritance; it has long been known that our environment is a large determining factor in our lives. Both have a powerful influence.

Another thing that is fairly common in the aftermath of suicide is a *panic attack*. With a panic attack, the individual is suddenly, usually without provocation, filled with waves of fear that last for a minute or two — but seem like hours. Panic attacks are spontaneous; they can occur anywhere or time — away from home or possibly just as you are trying to go to sleep. The panic feeling itself is frightening — and the fear of the panic returning causes great anxiety.

WHAT IS FEAR?

Some information about what actually is happening when you are afraid is helpful. The feeling of fear is awful, but all the other things that happen when we are afraid are *physiological effects of adrenaline in our bloodstream*. It is so frightening to be afraid that we don't notice the purely physical things that accompany fear. None of them are harmful:

- your hearts beats faster, sometimes skipping beats, and booming in your chest
- you break out in a sweat on your forehead and hands
- your skin may feel tingly
- you may feel as if a tight band is around your head
- your muscles knot up
- your stomach muscles contract
- your eyes see bright sparks
- you feel dizzy
- everything may go dark, and you fear passing out
- you feel nauseated

When you consider having all these physical reactions at once, you can see why the fear often increases. The best thing you can do is *talk to yourself — reassure yourself*. Tell yourself, "It's just adrenaline. It always goes away." Take deep breaths, and move your body to dissipate the adrenaline. It is a fact that adrenaline can only do so much physiologically to our bodies; there is a maximum amount of effect adrenaline can have. Consequently, the panic attack you have already experienced is probably the worst it will ever get.

Your anxiety and fear about the panic returning, however, are very uncomfortable. Fear is fed on anticipation so the best prescription for fear and panic is to *stay in the present*. People who are phobic get into a frightening circle described as "fear of the fear." The time when you are not panicking is spent worrying and fearing the panic will come back. So there is always fear. Don't ask yourself "what if" questions. Staying in the present is good grief advice as well. Ask yourself "Am I all right now?" Too often we catastrophize when we are grieving. We worry about the future, and feel we can't stand it. In fact, you are grieving because *the worst that could happen already has: some you love has died.*

SHOCK AND DENIAL

Denial is a *psychological* protective mechanism, just as shock is a *physiological* protective mechanism. Shock and denial will be your friends in the early months of grief. In suicide death there are two kinds of denial: denial before and denial after the suicide. Suicide survivors are victims in more than one sense. They are victims of the tragedy of death, but also victims of a society which left them unprepared for the events leading up to the death.

DENIAL BEFORE DEATH

Suicide has been so wrapped in secrecy, fear and superstition that even "well-known" facts about suicide are not known by the unsuspecting public. People instinctively know when things are not right, and most of you saw things you knew weren't right. The taboo has deprived us of information about mental illness; even the professionals who are meant to help us may not know more than we do.

In fact, most of us were raised with the "information" that "depression is normal" and that "everyone gets depressed." The word depression is misused. Everyone sometimes is unhappy, sad, forlorn, blue, miserable, or dismayed by the normal ups and downs of life. Depression is a brain disease involving an imbalance of the chemicals that regulate how we think, feel and behave. Most of us did not know that depression could kill until it happened in our families. In retrospect, most of us realized the one we loved was depressed. We often say things like, "I knew he was depressed, but I didn't know he was that depressed!"

Consequently, before the suicide, we were frightened when we heard statements about hopelessness and suicide. We were frightened into doing nothing. Because we didn't know what to do, we convinced ourselves that we hadn't heard or seen what we did and we "forgot" it — to protect ourselves from what was too awful to contemplate. This is the denial mechanism. We "forgot" and hoped for the best. *After* the suicide, all the things we "forgot" come tumbling out of our memory as things we *should* have known and *should* have done something about.

DENIAL AFTER DEATH

The worst has happened, and our first response is likely to be one of protest. "I don't believe it," or "It can't be true," may be our first reaction. This is denial after a suicide combined with shock. Shock is that physical reaction that makes us feel as if we are wrapped in cotton, that we are sleepwalking, and that makes our pain feel far away. Denial helps us tell our family and friends what happened, make arrangements for everyone to get home, plan a funeral, and meet and greet all the people who come.

It's the time when people sometimes say of us, "My, she's taking it so well." It seems if we manage to stand up and behave ourselves appropriately in public, some people want to think we are doing "so well." Shock and denial are protective; they help us get through these end-of-life rituals. More and more, since churches and synagogues support instead of punish, it *is* easier on us, and easier for our friends and relatives to rush to our side.

Many of you will have had this experience of support, but almost all of us have had at least a few bad experiences as well. Over and over we hear that gasp of shock from people when they hear it was suicide. Almost all of us have run into some awful boor who makes a really thoughtless or insensitive comment. We are suddenly sensitive to anything about suicide, and we become so sensitized that we suddenly realize how many television shows, movies and books utilize suicide as entertainment. A suicide is added to give a little "edge" or shock value to a story. We now realize that suicide isn't "entertaining" anymore.

There are stories run in the newspapers all over the country telling of ordinary and unknown people who kill themselves in grotesque ways. Maybe it was someone you loved who was written up this way, and your tragedy was spread all over the continent for the titillation of others. Suicides of unknown people are not usually news. Unless the suicide is by a well-known person, who has killed him or herself in a very spectacular and public manner, it is not news.

What helps you through all this horror is denial after the suicide death. Denial which helps us forget — while we are going on with our lives — because *we have to*. Most people feel as if they will completely fall apart, but almost none of us does, nor do we have the luxury to do so. We have jobs, children, spouses, parents, siblings and friends, and we have responsibilities to all of them. As hard as it is, most people find the routine of living helps them get through those first days that seem agonizingly long.

Most people don't realize that their "friends" — shock and denial — are helping them go on, and that these friends stay with them for many months. Shock and denial leave slowly and gradually. They often dump us unceremoniously into that raging river of grief, but they also help us get back out a tiny bit stronger for the effort. Each time it seems to take all our strength, but suddenly — it seems — we begin to see little signs of hope.

We look back and say, "It's been a month since it happened, and I can't believe I got through it!" It comes as a relief, and a little bit of pride of survivorship. It helps us up when we fall again and again into tears of despair. After our tears have helped relieve some of our emotions, we remember, "Well, I went on before." We compare and realize, "Well, if I did it then, I can do it again."

RELIEF

Who could be relieved when someone dies by suicide? You, for one. Because many of us lived under extreme tension with someone we loved who died, and since most of us did see signs of suicide or things that might have been signs of suicide, his or her death can be like the other shoe dropping. The anxiety is over. The worst thing we feared has finally happened, and we can be allowed a breath of relief.

It is not true that all people are ignorant of what is going on. There are those survivors who have dealt with the chronic mental illness of a loved one in the form of manic-depression and schizophrenia. These are terrible crippling diseases that can torment people for years. A small number of people with these illnesses kill themselves, and when they do, it is normal and natural for the survivors to feel relieved. They are relieved that a great and long ordeal has finally ended.

Some suffered so long watching someone they loved who was so ill, there is hardly any emotion left for grief. Most of the survivors have watched the illness turn someone they love into a stranger for whom they are responsible. There are physical illnesses, such as cancer, that cause people to say after the death comes, "It was a blessing." This is often true of the terrible "mental cancers" called manic-depression and schizophrenia.

This relief comes because your own stress is gone, but many people feel equally relieved that the suffering of someone they love has ended. Often we didn't realize how badly they were suffering, and only in retrospect do we know how they hurt. Many people feel guilt when they experience these normal feelings of relief. Relief is one of the only things in grief that feels good, so don't waste time and energy feeling guilty about a normal human reaction. Be as realistic as you can. As awful as it sounds to say it, for some survivors there are positive benefit — such as financial or emotional — when a long illness results in death. In other situations where alcohol or illegal drugs made the relationship a nightmare, the death may be a net benefit to family peace. There is nothing terrible about acknowledging it. This doesn't mean you are glad they are dead.

Again remember there are so many terrible things in the basketful of grief we carry that we would be foolish not to let ourselves feel the benefits of one of the few good things. In some relationships, so much attention had to be devoted to caring for someone with a chronic illness that all the others, including yourself, have been deprived. Of course it was done gladly, but don't ignore the bit of happiness that seeps through when you realize the potential for a new freedom.

DELAYED GRIEF

Some people were never allowed to grieve, or didn't allow themselves to grieve, and they carry their burdens as best they can. Sometimes when there is a suicide death in the family, small children are "protected" by lying to them, or forbidding them to talk about the person who died and/or their death. There is also a tendency for some people to put their grief "in the past" and not think about it. Some adults who grieve a suicide death try to shut things out in the past, and do their best to "carry on." Some other people seem to devote their lives to the past, and carry their pain with them all their lives. Delayed grief usually occurs when people try to stamp their pain down, but every time they stamp, it hurts more. Taking time to grieve may also be a luxury of the middle and wealthy classes. Everyone has to go on, but people in grinding poverty must go on for their very existence, or to sustain the existence of others.

After a suicide, some survivors act as if they can change the past. This results in the normal "what-iffing" and "if-onlys" people do so frequently after a suicide death. It is a necessary look at the past, but when it becomes exaggerated and excessive, grief may be delayed. Sometimes people hang onto their grief, feeling they deserve punishment for having failed the one who died. Some people, such as young children, who hadn't been allowed to grieve, carry their pain like a permanent ache. Delayed grief can be like carrying a rock everywhere one goes. Sometimes belated grief and tears can dissolve the "rock." (*Kristen and the Rock*, Karen Dahl, privately printed, 1984.) It hurts to carry these "rocks" from the past. A few people are permanently damaged by their delayed grief.

Other people store their grief away in a sealed compartment. There is a common belief that this sealing away of grief will greatly damage, if not destroy people. This isn't necessarily true. The brain has ways of protecting us, and this is one of them. If one thinks of the brain partly as a storehouse, it may be desirable to close off one "room." It doesn't necessarily prevent people from living productive and full lives; in fact, it may help them. It may be their only way of defending themselves. This is normal grief for many people.

Some people who use this way of sealing off their pain are afraid of what might happen if they "let go." Most of them have a vague dread of being overwhelmed — of being incapacitated by their grief if they "let it out." If this is your situation, ask yourself, "What is the worst that could happen?" You might completely go to pieces. What does that mean? Well, you might break down crying and sobbing, and find it hard to regain control. Has total loss of control ever happened to you before? No? Well then, it won't now. But what if you break down emotionally in front of someone else? What if you did? It would likely be a kind person who cares about you, and wouldn't think badly of you if you did. The fact is that the worst that could happen to you is that you would temporarily lose emotional control. That's not so terrible; if you have held all your grief in for months or years, you have a lot to cry about. You deserve to feel sorry for yourself.

You might begin by pouring out your grief and pain to your pastor or rabbi, a relative or friend. If you feel you can't do that, pour it all out on paper. Tell the person, or tell the piece of paper, the whole terrible story. Pour out all the things too terrible to talk about. Lose control, break down and cry. Maybe you are angry; you probably should be. Perhaps someone made you hide it all away when you were too little or weak to fight back. You have a right to be angry. Perhaps there are things you feel guilty about — perhaps you feel responsible in some way. Tell it all, or write it all. The worst that can happen is you will lose emotional control for awhile. That's not so awful; it probably has happened before in your life. It's only temporary; you always regain control. Almost everyone has experienced feeling better after a good cry, and you will too. If you are too fearful, or just can't do it, you may want to see a professional if your delayed grief is getting in the way of things you want to do in the present. It is never too late to grieve.

SLEEP, DREAMS AND VISIONS

It is not unusual to have difficulty sleeping for a few months after the suicide. Common problems are difficulty falling asleep, or falling asleep but waking early and being unable to go back to sleep. Some people see the death scene or other terrible things in their minds, which keep them from falling asleep. You may feel more tired than usual during the day, or have problems concentrating. Generally, these problems are worst in the first few months, and begin to go away six or seven months after the death. Not everyone has any or all of these problems, but they are normal and should not alarm you if they happen. (Remember that if any of these are extreme, long lasting, and you are unable to function, it can be major depression on top of your grief. See your doctor if this is the case.)

A majority of people dream about the person who died. The most common dream is that they didn't die. Very often the person who died will "come back" in the dream to reassure or to explain — sometimes that the death was all a mistake. People sometimes have dreams about the childhood of their loved one, and these dreams generally have the theme that the one you loved is still alive. There are also "second chance" dreams in which people dream they are rescuing their loved one in some way. Dreaming gradually recedes, and suicide survivors often report that their dreams change to "searching" themes. One may dream of a house, in which in every room they search, the loved one has just left — just when they are so close, they are lost again. Dreams rarely occur often, and dream activity recedes with time.

It is also fairly common, especially shortly after the death, to "forget they died." If the phone rings, you may think for a second that your loved one is calling you; you may find yourself setting a place at the table for them. You may "see" or "hear" them. Your memory may be so vivid that you see their face in someone who resembles them, or you may imagine you hear some distinctive sound they made coming in the house, or "hear" their voice. These "visions" rarely last more than a second or two, but it's enough to make you feel acute disappointment when reality makes you remember they are dead.

ANNIVERSARIES AND HOLIDAYS

If you read other books on grief, you will find there is a lot of talk about how badly you are going to feel on anniversaries and holidays. There is often a suggestion that supportive friends and relatives call you on anniversaries of the death, and other special times. Some people do cope by "storing up" their grief until the day, and letting it all out on the anniversary day. Many suicide survivors, however, have much more trouble with the *anticipation of the special day* than the day itself.

Survivors may start to fear and anticipate the anniversary date — even a month ahead of time, and it seems to get worse the nearer the day comes. But by the time it does come, many people have spent so much time anticipating and fearing the day that the anniversary itself is anti-climactic. With the passage of years, many survivors report a brief anticipation prior to the anniversary, but some feel guilty because they did not have this anxious anticipation, and even forgot the day. In fact, this is a sign of returning to normal, of not letting the terrible thing that happened in the past control the rest of your life.

Of course, holidays, birthdays and anniversaries will be very sad — especially for the first year as each milestone marking their lives passes without them. But these special days can begin to gather even more importance if, with the sadness and loss, you determine that the surviving members of your family must enjoy each other all the more because you now realize how important you are to each other.

When you find yourself dreading some holiday, remind yourself that *the worst that can happen already has happened.* The worst that can happen now is that you will have a very unhappy day — you may collapse in sobbing and feel you will never get over it. But this has happened to you before, and you did get through it — and you will again. You might try something called challenging: try to imagine what the day will be like — try to make yourself feel the worst you can. Usually when you try to make yourself feel a particular way, you can't. Usually if you tell yourself to "Do your worst, I don't care," it has the effect of strengthening you, because you are accepting the fact that you *can* take what comes.

As painful as it may seem, anniversaries and holidays are good occasions for remembering the person you loved who died. It might seem too painful, but many families have discovered that a time set aside for everyone's memories will bring back some of the happiness of the past through the pain of the present. A lot of people like to have pictures around, and "talk to them." Other people put their pictures away for awhile; the reminder is just too painful. A lot of people wear an old shirt or sweater that belonged to their loved one who died.

You might make their favorite dinner on their birthday, or make a donation in their memory. Of course you may shed a tear or many. These are examples of the only way you can still "do" something for someone you love who died — and you will discover it also is doing something for yourself. You need memories — good and bad — because they are a living monument you will always have. You can gather memories from other people in the family, from the loved one's friends, and add these to yours. As long as you live, someone you loved will still be alive in your memory.

CHAPTER 5

ANGER, BLAME AND GUILT

We often don't stop to realize it, but another thing that feels good, in moderation, is anger. To feel anger, to scream and accuse, helps us "get it out of our system." For a long time, people have realized that bottling up anger only hurts us, but to sit quietly and hold our anger inside a little helps us in the same way. Nursing our anger — if we don't do it too much — is sensing the injustice done to us "after all we did" for someone who has left us so brutally.

ANGER

Many of us cry in anguish, "How could he do this to me?" We are not ready yet to realize that he was probably in such emotional pain that he *couldn't* think of you, or if he did, he thought you would be better off! Anger is energy. Angry people often have a tremendous amount of strength. To a certain extent, we can let anger's energy work for us. To tackle cleaning out the garage in a fury of energy helps us "get *it* out of our systems," and has the positive benefit of "finally getting that job done."

BLAME

Anger becomes dangerous when we use its energy to hurt other people. One of our defenses against painful angry feelings is to blame other people for the suicide. Seldom is there a clear-cut villain we can blame for "causing" the suicide, but any person, group or even a corporation is a candidate for blame. It is most often anyone near us, and we usually want it to appear that it is "they" who are the bad people and "we" the good people. It is so easy to blame, because all of us are so fallible. It is easy to blame because all of us are imperfect and guilty of many things. We often are angry and placing blame to put distance between us and that desolate feeling of isolation and aloneness —where each of us has to face the reality that someone we loved has died, and there is *never* anything *any* of us can *ever* do about it. Only with death are the words "forever," "ever" and "never" true. This is the desolation of grief. There are no second chances. In this life, they are beyond us *forever*, and the terrible reality of grief is our knowledge that we will *never* see them again on this earth. *No wonder we are angry!*

The person we are most likely to be angry with is the person who died, and we innately realize how silly this is. They *are* gone, and we can't *ever* reach them here again. Mercifully, they can't hear us; their pain is gone. But *their pain has been transferred to us*, and one way of dealing with this pain is through anger.

As healthy as it is to feel and release anger, we might think about what anger really is: one writer said at the most basic level, we become angry because *we did not get our way*. Things did not turn out the way we wanted them to, and now there is *never* any hope they will. Not only has someone we loved died, but so have all our dreams for them — and us. This is a lot to be angry about. We need to try to remember to let the steam off our anger harmlessly, and not vent it on other people who may be feeling just as bad as we are. It hurts us just as much being angry at really "bad" people, because we, not they, feel the brunt of our anger.

Anger and other emotions are neither good nor bad; they just are. We may not be able to control how we *feel*, but we can control what we *do*. We might feel like driving the car at eighty miles an hour, but we keep ourselves from doing it by remembering our responsibilities. We might want to scream and break things, but we control ourselves. We may want to accuse and blame others for the death and our pain, but we have to control our tongues and remember the parable that reminds us that "he who is without blame may throw the first stone." Anger is normal. Feel it, feel its cleansing fire, and control yourself until it burns itself out and you feel better.

UNPOPULAR AND GUILTY VICTIMS

The public stigma on suicide creates a perception that we and our loved ones are "unpopular" and "guilty" victims. This has prevented suicide survivors from banding together in strength to throw off the stigma. Since 1978 about 200 support groups for suicide survivors have sprung up in the United States and Canada. All of them are individual efforts with no united national group to give advice, guidance and support. No national celebrity suicide survivor has put more than token effort into suicide reduction. There are no telethons raising millions of dollars every year.

By contrast, a group that has "popular" and "innocent" victims is Mothers Against Drunk Driving (MADD). They richly deserve their success, but suicide survivors can only envy them their strong national headquarters, and chapters in each of the United States and Canadian provinces during the same period our individual and isolated efforts have struggled to bring suicide survivors together. MADD has permanently changed the way people feel about drunk driving. That needs doing about suicide as well.

SOCIETY BRANDS SURVIVORS GUILTY

After a suicide, virtually the first message that gets through is how guilty we *must* feel. Combined with this, is the message of how ashamed we *must* feel. People say, "Oh, that poor family; they *must* feel terribly guilty." Others say, "Oh, it *must* be awful for them, dealing with *all that guilt*." What do they mean? Why *must* we feel guilty and have "all that guilt?" How do they know how guilty you feel? Would they assume you *must* feel guilty if someone you loved had died from cancer? No. And it is not that they are bad or unkind people; they have inherited the centuries-old condemnation of suicide that says only "bad" people kill themselves, and, consequently, they *must* come from "bad" (dysfunctional) families who have "all that guilt."

This is the public assumption that suicide survivors are guilty in a way that other people are not. This assumption, from the Dark Ages, that we should have some brand to show people our guilt and shame for having a suicide in the family lives on. Unfortunately, the stigma has affected us so much that we often accept this brand, or place it there ourselves. But this is not fair. You are a good person who did your best, loved your most, and had a terrible tragedy happen.

REAL GUILT

This is not to say that you don't feel guilty; you wouldn't be human if you didn't feel guilty after the death of someone you loved. This is *real* guilt. In this life, there is no second chance for us to do things we should or could have done differently, nor can we call back unkind or angry words, nor change decisions. Resolving real guilt is one of the important jobs of grief. Our family and friends may try to comfort us by saying, "Don't feel guilty." This is well-intended, but, painful as it is, real guilt has to be looked at, admitted and grieved over. The fact that you do feel guilty proves you are a good person; the fact that you have not always been able to do the right things, say the best things, and make the correct decisions proves you are human.

Your intentions were always good, but you weren't always good. Part of the work of grief is to be able to look at the things you were guilty of, cry over them, and gain strength to be better after you have healed. And you will heal; *you have to*. There are some people who say you will be consumed with guilt and shame the rest of your life. That's nonsense! You need to gradually switch emphasis from your real guilt, and remember how many times you were forgiven, and how much you were loved by someone you loved who died. If there is one incident that seems too terrible to think about, force yourself to think of similar situations in which you *did* do what you now think was right. Think of all the times you said, thought, and decided things that *didn't* result in suicide.

Suicide is not a rational or clearly thought-out action. If suicide is any kind of a "choice," it is a coerced choice, in which someone you loved was unable to see alternatives and consequences. Having said that, it is nonetheless true that it is the person who died who decided *when* all else had failed, *when* everything he or she tried hadn't worked, and *when* the pain was too much to bear anymore.

WHAT-IFFING GUILT

Because someone you loved didn't *have* to die as a result of a terminal physical cause, we are prone to attribute omnipotence to ourselves. We should have known; we should have done things differently, if we had only done one thing extra, we think *"then* they would still be alive." Whatever you did or didn't do just before their death, you had done or hadn't done many times before. If you were mad at them, you had been mad at them many times before when they hadn't killed themselves. If you were gone from home when they killed themselves, you had been gone from home endless times when they didn't kill themselves. If you failed to say,"I love you," before they died, you need to remember we don't go around expressing our love every minute of the day to those we love, and take for granted they will be there.

A certain amount of "what-iffing" and "if-only" thinking is a good process to help you come to grips with the fact that you probably did do all you reasonably could. We tend to idealize the dead, but we must remember that depressed people can be very unreasonable, and oftentimes downright difficult to live with. Depressed people tend to have two sides to their personalities: 1) depressed and dependent, unhappy and clinging, and/or 2) irritable, angry and so touchy one can hardly talk to them. One has the feeling it is necessary to walk on eggshells to keep from "setting them off." People who have manic-depression or schizophrenia can be very difficult to live with, which is an understatement given the severity of the symptoms of these brain diseases. They do and say bizarre things, are abnormally suspicious, and although they do not do it on purpose, can destroy relationships, jobs, school or lead to bankruptcy.

At a certain point, you need to look back realistically at the person who died, and remember how he or she actually was before death. The loved one certainly hadn't the saintly image you may be trying so hard to impose on yourself. You likely are remembering happier times before they were so sick and upset. You need to remember all the things you tried, all the times you were loving and patient, all the times you wracked your brain for one more thing that might help, all the times you gave things up for someone you loved, and nothing worked. That's right — nothing worked — and your loved one died.

It's *normal* to feel you will never be happy again, but you will. It's *normal* to wish you could just crawl in a hole, and give up, but you won't. It's *normal* to doubt your ability to relate to the rest of your family and friends, but you will. It's *normal* to think if you had only done or said things differently, then that loved one would still be alive, but he or she wouldn't. It's *normal* to hurt so much you think you won't ever recover, but you will. You will *because you have to;* you will because down the road, the future will beckon you to come back.

GRIEF AND POWER

Things did not turn out the way we wanted, and we are angry and desperately hurt by it. One person [1] has pointed out an important distinction about our personal power. He says that in any situation in life there are some things that a person can do, and some things that are up to others, or to outside factors, or to chance. We can set goals and do our best, but we cannot, by our own power, make things turn out the way we want.

To imagine that the entire outcome is up to us, *that we have the power* to determine what will happen or, in retrospect *that we did have the power* to determine what happened in the past, is illusory or imaginary power. One can set goals and do one's best, but one cannot by one's own power ensure success. When you go over and over pre-death circumstances and events, searching for acts of omission or commission that you believe caused the suicide, you are attempting to maintain an imaginary power.

We do not have a power that somehow says the past will be magically changed if we only do enough penance, or refuse to believe the present. You may say that you don't really believe your loved one can be brought back by your efforts, but the danger is that if you remain at the "what-iffing" and "if-only" stage, you will *act* as if you have this power, and you will waste your energies in a vain attempt at having a second chance.

Some people take the energy which had been expended in real relationships (real power) and shift it toward maintaining a relationship with the deceased (illusory power). The fear is that without the illusory power, there will be no power at all.(1) The fear may be that living in the past is the only way to stay with someone who died. While we cannot bring the person back, and while there are no second chances with the person who died, there are many second chances with the living — with others who need and want us here and now. This is where your real power lies. It's hard to come back to the present, and to face the future, but that too, is the work of grief. You will come back to the present and the future, not only because you have to, but because you will want to.

CHAPTER 6

WHO DO YOU TELL? WHAT DO YOU SAY?

Because there have been hundreds of years of stigma and taboo on suicide, the simple matter of notifying people of the death poses the question of what do you tell them? It isn't just at the time of the death, but in the future. Who needs to know? What should we tell people? Which of the relatives should we tell? What about children? In all cases *tell the truth*. Often you have no alternative, but where you do have a choice, you will do harm to yourself and other members of your family if you try to "hush it up." There is nothing so awful that mankind hasn't seen before. The suicide will be a terrible shock to your friends and family, but get the information out fast so you won't have to go on and on telling people who haven't heard.

If you are worried about gossip and rumors, realize that the truth is the best way to squelch rumors. If you try to make up some "cover story" it will be more difficult. Your self- consciousness will probably show and only make people suspicious or pity you if they know the truth. Let other people help you. Their shock and surprise is their problem; you don't have to worry about shielding them. Many suicide survivors report that their friends and family rushed to help them, but people can't do this for you if they sense they are being held at a distance by a lie.

LET YOUR CLERGY HELP YOU

It may not seem so at the time, but if your pastor or rabbi discusses the suicide at the funeral service, they are doing you a favor. He or she is telling a large group of people the awful fact that is so hard for you to repeat over and over. Clergy who deal compassionately with the suicide in the funeral service are also setting a wonderful example of support for you. Your friends and acquaintances can learn from them how to help you.

If your clergy *isn't* helpful, or condemns your loved one, look around and realize that the majority of religious people today are not like that. Obviously, this is easier said than done. But remember that people change churches and religions all the time. You don't have to associate with people who say awful things about you and about someone you loved who died. It hurts terribly if your clergy condemns your loved one, you and your family. Good and kindly religious people don't do this.

TELLING CHILDREN

It is plain to see that your friends and people at work need to know about the suicide in your family, but little children? Yes, they need to know the truth as well. Being the only one who doesn't know, places your child in a terrible position. Young children are smarter than we sometimes think; they certainly are sensitive and tuned to the currents and undercurrents in their homes. They know when something is wrong; they often have seen things — sometimes they have seen the body. You can't turn around and tell them it was an accident. This could cause a terrible rupture in your relationship. If you lie to them about something as important as a death in the family, it can hurt them in the short and long run. All the children in your neighborhood know, and if you don't tell your child they will. Children need to be told by people who love them.

After a suicide in your family, you need to call the principal, the counselor, or your child's teacher, and tell them of this terrible thing that has happened. The school needs to be aware that your children are grieving, and it needs to hear the facts from you. Children often think that if they just go back to school and say nothing, somehow things will be okay. They are always self-conscious, and may be doubly so when there is a death in the family. As bad as it is, it certainly is better if you tell the school than if it hears it through rumor and speculation. Your children may not like your doing this, but you must. If the school people know the facts from you, they can help the rest of the students.

Your child's friends need accurate information so they can befriend as best they can. They also need to understand about grief and be prepared for some of the perfectly normal, but scary things that happen to their grieving friend. There just isn't any way you can take the pain of grief away from children, but you can make it worse by closing them out.

When a student kills him or herself, it is a good idea to have some kind of intervention by counselors and mental health people in handling shock and grief. Sometimes, however, when a student kills him or herself people from outside come into a school and act as if the whole student body is somehow is at risk for suicide. Schools have been advised by "experts" that it is dangerous to talk to young people about suicide.

But imagine the fear, worry and hurt of a young person who knows what happened but is swept adrift in a ocean of silence. Young people see the fear in the adults around them, and they hear the whispers used to talk about suicide. The majority of students in a large school won't know the person who died, and they will be surprised, fearful and shocked. They need information, reassurance and an explanation of how suicide happens. They don't need to hear hysterical predictions that they can somehow be lured or enticed into killing themselves.

IF YOU HAVE ALREADY LIED

If you have already lied to your child or children, you should make it right — now. You need to get him, her or them with you, and say you thought you were doing the right thing when you told them the death was an accident, but you realize now they need to know the truth. Apologize to them for lying, and explain how you thought it was for the best at the time. Tell them simply what the cause of death was, and then answer their questions. Be prepared for them to be angry with you for lying. It can be a valuable lesson for them to see that adults sometimes do lie, and that this is the way people correct lies. You and they will probably be relieved to get it out in the open.

But surely one shouldn't tell really young children. Perhaps not. Babies and two-year-olds need to understand that the person who died is gone permanently. Three and four-year-olds need to hear the truth simply, because if you don't tell them, they will find out, and it may be in an awful way. Obviously, little children don't need every single detail, but they need to know that the person did it to him or herself, and how, with a simple explanation of why. They need to know that some people feel so badly inside themselves that sometimes they kill themselves, because they can't think of any other way of taking the hurt away. They need to know that people can be sick in their emotions as well as in their bodies.

But how can you explain the method of death that was chosen? There are so many guns on television that it is not difficult for young children to understand a gun death. They probably have seen suicide deaths on television. It is harder to explain when the method of death was hanging, poison or one of the bizarre methods some people use to kill themselves. Be truthful. Tell them you don't know why he or she picked that method. Children can get funny and unrealistic ideas, and need to be assured that they can ask questions and have honest answers. As they grow older, they will want to understand the death in more detail. Answer questions simply, accurately and as they come up. *There is nothing too awful to talk about; everything in the world has happened before.*

Honesty about emotions is just as important. If you are angry, it's all right to let them know that. They probably are too. Don't "spare your children." You need to cry, they need to cry, and they need to see you cry. They despair and you despair sometimes. They need help from you to understand that these emotions are temporary. They may come and go, but they are a normal part of grieving. They need to know they won't always feel this way; *you* need to know you won't always feel this pain.

TELLING EVERYONE

At first it seems you have told everyone, and that everybody knows. Even in small towns this isn't necessarily true — that "everyone knows." There are some people who should know who may not. That friend who hasn't called you probably doesn't know yet. We all have acquaintances and friends who we don't see very often, and they have other sets of acquaintances and friends. We assume the news of the suicide is going to "spread like wild fire," but that often isn't the case. People are gone when things happen, they have their own problems that distract them; they just simply may not have heard about it. Whatever the reason, you will run into people who don't know. It happens less and less as time goes on, but you probably will run into people six months or a year afterwards who don't know that someone you loved has died.

It is a good idea to decide on a short explanation of what happened, and memorize it, if necessary. Some examples: "It was a terrible shock to us, but he killed himself." — "She died; she took her own life in January." — "We didn't realize how depressed he was, and he killed himself." Make it short and fast, and be prepared for the other person's shock. It's not fair, but suicide is a shocking death, and one of the extra burdens suicide survivors have is dealing with other people's gasps of shock or disapproval when they hear the news.

Another matter is whether to tell the method of death in the explanation. An example, "It was a terrible shock; he shot himself." People are curious about methods of suicide, and some boors come right out and ask what method the victim chose. To prevent speculation, it probably is better to tell the method. If it was a very public suicide, they will already know. Some people may blurt out, "Was she on drugs?" or make some other tactless comment. It is easier said than done, but try not to get upset by all this. Some of these people mean well, and the others are not worth getting upset about. Still other people will be genuinely concerned for you, and you will need to say something soothing to them. Can you believe this? You are the one who has had the tragedy, and you have the extra burden of telling people, "That's all right; I know it's a shock." *We have to take care of them before they can turn around to console us!*

TELLING PEOPLE IN THE FUTURE

Who should we tell and who needs to know? Your family and people who marry into your family need to know about the suicide. They need to know that there is depression, manic-depression or schizophrenia in the family, the same way they need to know if there is diabetes or heart disease. It is part of our health history. We need to know about the illnesses in our families so we can spot them in time in the future. Couples need to know the family medical history when planning children. There is nothing that foredooms you or your family because there has been a suicide, or more than one.

If you meet someone at a coffee counter, and visit over lunch, that person doesn't need to know your whole history. If you're a widow, you can just say you're single. If one of your children died, and you're asked how many children you have, just say the remaining or original number. People you meet casually don't need to know about this particular tragedy in your life. If that person subsequently becomes your friend, however, you will need to tell your new friend and explain the circumstances. People who care about you need to know. The suicide of someone you loved is just too big an event in your life for your friends not to know.

One final warning! You will run into any number of people who will boorishly foist on you their *half-baked* opinions about suicide. There are professional people who have *half-baked* ideas about suicide, and who may press their pet views on you, often insisting you and your whole family need counseling. You just don't need, and you don't have to tolerate, unsolicited opinions and advice about this tragedy in your life.

CHAPTER 7

RELATIONSHIPS

One of the biggest lessons death teaches us is to value our friends and family. They are always our best support. Everything is so difficult, but one of the worst things you can do for each other is to try to maintain a "stiff upper lip" for the sake of others. Parents must see their children cry; how else can you know when to give them comfort? Children need to see their parents' grief; how else will they know how deeply you care?

Brothers and sisters need the example of their parents' grief to learn how to manage theirs. Husbands and wives often try to "hold themselves together" for the other's sake. Your relatives — your aunts and uncles and grown sisters and brothers need to know how and when to help you. Some relatives and friends who didn't know your loved one well will grieve more for you and your pain. Our friends want to help us, and the very difficult thing is that we have to let them. We are so used to being self-sufficient — so reluctant to "impose on anyone" that sometimes we don't give our relatives and friends the opportunity of helping us.

Another thing you need to remember is that there are never ideal circumstances in families. In some families there are real breaks between people. Sometimes people will be brought together by tragedy, but more often the problems in relationships that were there before the death are still there, and perhaps they become worse. In the real world, death puts a great strain on relationships, and the strengths and weaknesses that were there before will still be there. Many people become better and stronger because of tragedy. But if you were on the verge of divorce before the suicide, you still are. If your marriage was so-so, you will still have a lot of ups and downs with your partner. If your marriage and other relationships were good and strong, you will reap those rewards in comfort and love.

CONTEST FOR WORST PLACE

You will hear many people say that the worst thing that can happen is the death of a child. Not always. Couples who have good marriages often find great comfort in having each other. Facing death forces many people to revise their priorities. Death forces a change in basic values. The basic value is being alive! It can cause some things thought so important to be revised. We can start to ask this question: "Tomorrow, will this seem worth making an issue of now?" A lot of things we get upset about seem unimportant when put to this test.

Is the death of a child worse? Think of the widow or widower left alone, or left alone with young children. Think of the seventy-year-old mother whose forty-five-year-old son kills himself. What about his children and wife? What about his brothers and sisters scattered across the country? Think of the twenty-year-old widower. How can his parents comfort him; how does he feel about his in-laws? How do they feel about him? Think of the divorced couple whose child kills himself? Think of the thirty-year-old brother whose sister kills herself? Think of every imaginable relationship in suicide death, and you have the real world of suicide grief. When it is someone *you* love, it is the worst!

It may not seem so now, but when you realize you can still think and care about other suffering people, when you learn that you can still reach out, that you can still sympathize with someone else, when you can still see people worse off than you are, then acceptance and return to life after suicide begins. Beginnings and endings are the circle of life. The beginning, however, is only the first step of our return to our new lives. Your life will never be entirely the same again because someone you loved has died — has died in a ghastly way, and there is just no quick route back to life without your loved one. The hole left in our lives after the death of someone we loved seems so huge that all we can do at first is step around it. This is why the relationships we have in our lives are so important.

This is why the demands on us to go on are so important. And we go on because we *have to*. Use your families and friends for help. Depend on them, rely on them; ask them for what you need. Then let them depend on you, rely on you; give *them* what they need. When you learn that even in this terrible grief you can still give and that you get help while you give it, you will have learned what is best about people and how they survive. *We get help and we give it — and we get help by giving it.*

RELATIONSHIPS HAVE UNIQUE PROBLEMS

Whether you grieve deeply or not at all depends on the relationship you had with the person who killed him or herself. It is always assumed that the closer in blood relationship one is to the person who died, the more deeply one will grieve, and the further away from blood relationship, the less one will grieve. This is generally true, but there are many exceptions. For example, it is wrong to assume that a person is grieving less because he or she was "only" a friend, or "only" an aunt or uncle. It is wrong to assume that siblings or spouses or anyone else will automatically grieve deeply.

A long-time friend of someone who killed himself may be closer to the person than a sister who is fifteen years older and lives across the country. That sister cares, but may never have had the time it takes to maintain a close and intimate relationship because of distance and time. A wife may not always grieve a husband's death. He may have been an abusive alcoholic for years, and she, understandably, may feel only relief after his suicide. These examples serve to show only that one should not assume the degree of grief is the same for everyone — even in the same family or in close relationships. The point is, don't feel guilty for what you are or what you feel. There are no right or wrong feelings, just right or wrong actions. If you are grieving a little less than someone else in your family, let them know they can lean on you a little bit more.

PARENT SURVIVORS OF A YOUNG CHILD

Popular and professional literature often assumes that the death of a child is the worst grief that can occur, and that the probability of recovery from this grief is dubious at best. This assumption further implies that this desperate grief occurs only with the death of a *young* child. This assumption that parents of a child grieve more minimizes the grief of other people grieving the suicide death of their sibling, parent or grandparent. It minimizes the grief of spouses, fiancees, or people living together. Other neglected grievers are grandparents, friends, and other relatives. Suicide grief is worst when it happens to you when someone you love has died.

Having said this, parents probably are unique in feeling more responsible for a child who dies than when someone else dies. Parents have the whole life history of their child to review for things that might have, or should have been done differently. Like every other griever, they have to face the irrevocability of the loss. They have the added burden of bearing the blame of people who say they are a sick family that somehow contributed to the suicide. Blame is especially placed on busy, ambitious, career-oriented parents who move a lot. They are regarded as parents who care more for their careers and possessions than for their children. These individuals are not granted the assumption that someone in their family was very sick and died, and that the rest of the family is well — the assumption they would be granted if it had been a cancer death.

Parents who face the suicide of their child hear dire predictions for their marriage. They hear that the divorce rate after the death of a child is anywhere from 60 to 90 percent. The 90 percent figure is questionable if for no other reason than not that many people can *afford* a divorce. The 60 percent figure is not particularly surprising as about 50 percent of all married people divorce anyway. On the other hand, if you are a single divorced parent, the likely assumption is that your child killed him or herself because of a broken family. The deck is stacked so you can't win either way. The fact is, the kind of marriage you have going into the suicide death grieving period predicts the way you and your spouse will grieve together.

If your marriage was on the brink of divorce before the death, the extra pressure of grief may well cause you to separate. If you have a close, helpful and loving relationship, you will probably pull together and deepen your relationship. When people say the death of a child is worse, they don't take into account the fact that couples have each other, whereas, for example, a spouse is left alone or with small children. But there is no better or worse in grief, it is all bad. When it happens to *you*, it is the worst.

PARENT SURVIVORS OF A GROWN CHILD

Elderly parents of grown children who kill themselves have different problems from parents of young children who die by suicide. The parents of a young suicide most often have other young children, and they must cope with their grief at the same time they have to guide their other children in their grief. Parents, being human, often want time out from parenting their other children, and it is not unusual for a family to drift in their own ways for awhile. People are resilient, and this muddling through things often works out well. The ideal parent, of course, would grieve deeply, and at the same time be the fully nurturing mom or dad they've always been expected to be. Unfortunately, there are no ideal parents.

Families, like marriages, will tend to be the same after a suicide as they were before. If they were close and talked a lot with each other, or if there were substantial problems in the family leading to a lack of communication, those same frameworks will still be there. Most families pull together in one way or another. After a suicide is not the time for telling parents and families how much better other families are.

An older or elderly parent who has a child who kills him or herself, has different problems and sets of relationships. The parent is more likely to be single or widowed and living alone. Consequently, the feelings of desolation and loneliness may be greater because of physical isolation. These parents may have longer memories to cherish of their children, but they have a shorter time to recover and appreciate them than young parents do. These parents who are closer to their own deaths, often feel it is unfair for their children to die first. In these days of long and healthy lives, children are expected to grieve for their parents, not the other way around.

GRANDPARENTS AND IN-LAWS

Grandparents have special problems surrounding the suicide of a grandchild. They often have a double grief; they grieve not only for their grandchild, but for the grief of their child. Many times they are a stabilizing influence for their children, because they have had more experience of great loss. They will put aside their own grief, and rush to help their children with theirs. They do it lovingly and willingly, but their sacrifice should be noted and appreciated.

Older or elderly parents whose grown child dies by suicide may have problems with the remaining in-law spouse and vice versa. Sometimes there has been friction with the in-laws before the death, and it is increased afterwards. There may be mutual accusations between them and the spouse. Even where there aren't bad feelings, a spouse may move to another city or state after the death. Or, after some time, the spouse may remarry. In any or all of these situations there may be problems for the grandparents in seeing their grandchildren, and this is felt as a deep loss by them.

The worst situation occurs when there is hostility between the remaining spouse and the in-laws. The spouse may refuse to let the grandparents see the children, and there may not be much they can do about it. One avenue they can try is to find an intermediary such as a mutual friend, relative or a pastor or rabbi who can try to find some guidelines and rules for visitation. Going through the courts to resolve this problem is not uncommon any more. When the remaining spouse moves to a different city or state, the grandparents will have to reconcile themselves to the fact that they will see their grandchildren only on short visits. Often grandparents cannot afford to travel and the relationship has to be maintained by phone and letters. When widowed spouses remarry, it might not be unusual for grandparents to feel resentful. Nothing can replace children, but people do find new spouses. If you do find yourself resentful, try to realize where your resentment is coming from, and do your best to like the new partner. It may be your only alternative for a harmonious relationship with your grandchildren.

SPOUSES

When a spouse kills him or herself, a great deal depends on the age of the remaining spouse and the relationship they had with each other. Wives and husbands, as well as people who were living together, have a wide variety of relationships with each other. Most spouses left behind will be widows, because more men kill themselves than women do. Consequently, a great deal of emphasis is placed on the problems of widows, and widowers find less support for themselves. This is because there are fewer suicide survivor widowers than widowers from other deaths. The problems of spouses, however, are generally the same, and be assured that what follows applies to men as well as women.

Generally, younger spouses recover and remarry rather quickly — probably because they are more resilient, forward-looking and stronger. Initially, however, because of their youth, they may be more shocked and overwhelmed by the thought of the future, and have less financial resources. The twenty-six-year-old widow of a bus driver left with four children is in a different situation than that of a forty-year-old electrical engineer who is left with a house and four children after his wife's suicide. Remarriage at older ages is never simple due to difficulties of blending families, and simply because there aren't very many marriageable people available.

Widows and widowers, even in marriages which they thought were equal, discover after a suicide how many important things the other spouse had taken care of, and a host of little things which had been completely taken for granted. Financial resources always make a tremendous difference regardless of age. A young widower may have parents he can turn to for financial aid; a middle-aged widow may have to turn to welfare. With so many mixed marriages, a widow may not be able to get social security for her children because they were not legally adopted by her husband. In one very narrow situation, a widow can be denied social security for her children unless she can prove the suicide was an accident!

The relationship of the couple before the death determines how or whether the remaining partner will grieve. If there was a very loving relationship, though it may also have had lots of stress in the relationship, there will be genuine feelings of loss and grief for the surviving spouse. There may be very little or no grief if the couple had been just barely getting along, or even hostile. In these unhappy marriages, survivors may feel a good deal of relief. They may also, however, grieve for the lost dream and hope of a happy marriage. In some situations, where, for example, the person who died had depression and alcoholism for a long time, the death — although not longed for — may produce a positive benefit for the remaining family. There had been someone who was very sick in their family who died, and after the death they were able to start fresh to build on their strengths.

SEPARATED COUPLES

Sometimes suicides occur after a couple has separated or divorced. In some cases, the remaining spouse often grieves for that part of the marriage that was good — that person he or she originally loved. It is not uncommon for separated people to feel that if they had only stayed and tried harder, the suicide would have been prevented. Some relationships had so little left in them at the end, the spouse mourns more the loss of the dream — the dream that things would turn out all right — or return to the way they used to be. Sometimes when the divorce is long past when the suicide occurs, the remaining partner will have no grief at all, but will be concerned for their children's grief. These parents conscientiously respect the relationship their children had, and will try to help their children mourn.

The problems in-laws have go both ways after a suicide. There may be friction between spouses and in-law parents. In life, there are some people who are just plain hard to get along with, and sometimes they are in-laws. Some grandparents, or some spouses, were cranky, selfish and disagreeable people before the suicide, and remain so after it. The remaining in-laws may have tried everything to get along with them to no avail. The temptation will be great to sever the relationship. Where there are grandchildren, the temptation should be resisted because children often see a different side of people than adults.

A different situation prevails when there are no children to tie in-laws together. There often has been a loving relationship between in-laws which may be continued and strengthened even if there is a remarriage. Where the relationship has been strained and still is, the time is ideal to go separate ways. Even where there was a loving and supportive relationship between them and their in-laws, in the case of very young widows or widowers, they often drift away to begin new lives unencumbered by the past in-laws they didn't know well. A nineteen-year-old widow or a twenty-one-year-old widower deserves the chance to recover and begin anew with the blessings of in-laws. This is not to say that relationships should be severed, but only that, realistically in these cases, it is not unusual that in-law relationships fade away after a death when there are no children.

UNMARRIED COUPLES

Unmarried partners will have the same problems as spouses, and more. After the suicide of one of a couple living together, the remaining partner may be in a difficult legal position. Without a will, he or she is not the legal heir or partner of the person who died, and if the in-laws decide to exclude them, there is not much that can be done. It is easier if there was a good relationship, and the family includes the friend or fiancee left behind. More and more frequently, one does see a friend or fiancee listed in the obituary as a survivor. It is a dubious position to be in, however, and roommates, close friends, partners and fiancees are often the neglected grievers. This may be especially so when the couple was gay or lesbian.

YOUNG, TEENAGE AND OLDER CHILDREN

Young children, teenage children, and older children have different needs and capabilities. Young children tend to be neglected in the urgency of the aftermath of suicide, but they must be remembered quickly. They do not have the life experience to understand what has happened, and need information and reassurance. Everyone needs practical help after a death, but children especially need to understand what has happened, and need help in dealing with their friends and school. Children's friends do not call on them or send flowers when someone dies. Very young children may not really grasp the magnitude of what has happened, and may appear to chatter quite indifferently about the suicide. It is not unusual to hear a child say, "My daddy killed himself," as if it were ordinary conversation. Children may go around saying it freely to their friends. Their natural inclination to be open could be copied by grown-ups. Young children need simple, accurate information, with more details provided as they grow older and want more information.

Teenage suicide survivors are familiar with the family situation, and have a more complete grasp of the implications of the death. Many parents report their teenagers just don't want to, or won't talk about the suicide. Teenagers experience a great deal of self-consciousness, and they are often very, very embarrassed by the suicide. They need to receive concerned care, and to hear that they can talk about it when they want to. They also need a good role model in their family who talks in a normal way about the person who died and how much they are missed. When a person dies, it is *not* normal to have absolute silence about the fact. Suicide is too big an event to be undigested and ignored. If the school does not know about the suicide, a caring adult ought to inform it so allowances can be made for a temporary loss of concentration, a drop in grades, or a change in behavior. The teenager who is informed about the suicide, and about his or her part in the reorganization of the family — the teenager who is involved in plans for the future and has open communication, will get along very well.

Older children, in their twenties on up, tend to pull together for the sake of their parents when one of their siblings dies. Older children's needs often are neglected during the funeral period, and they may not be able to realize their own grief until they are back in their own homes. It is a great shock when one of your brothers or sisters kills themself. It is a terrible shock. Siblings expect their parents to die eventually, but not one of themselves! Often the sibling who kills him or herself lives far away, and there may be a great deal of unreality about the death. They are used to not seeing that member of the family and it is easy to "forget" they have died. If people are separated by great distances, they know there is the *possibility* of seeing each other, even if it is remote. But when one of them dies, they are removed from the earth! The possibility is gone. Older children grieve according to the closeness of the sibling who died. There are exceedingly close families, and those that tend to spin off and go their own ways. Older children have a lifetime of memories with their brothers and sisters, and their grief should not be minimized.

CHAPTER 8

RECOVERING AND GOING ON

The biggest need people have in grief is to be reassured. Reassurance is a guide that helps us gauge ourselves; to compare ourselves with a norm or standard. Being with other suicide survivors helps break down the isolation and fear we have when we are alone. Your difficulty in going through your grief, and getting back to your "new normal," may depend on the kind of messages you hear. If someone tells you immediately after the suicide that, "This is something so terrible you will never get over it," it can become a terrible self-fulfilling prophecy. On the other hand, your outcome may be very different if the message you hear is, "Yes, this is terrible, and you probably feel you won't ever get over it, but you will. It's hard for you to believe right now, but many people have done it, and so can you."

SUPPORT GROUPS FOR SUICIDE SURVIVORS

One of the most helpful things you can do for yourself is to attend a grief group for suicide survivors — if you are lucky enough to have one in your city. In a group you can talk to other survivors and compare your situation with theirs. We need to have our pain acknowledged, and to be supported by others. At the same time we are receiving support, we discover we can also give help to others. Support groups are based on this principle — that one gets help by giving it.

Self-help groups are divided two ways. First, they are divided as to whether the group is for a temporary problem, like grief, or for chronic problems, such as having a retarded child. Secondly, grief groups fall into closed or open groups. Closed groups work well in small communities where there aren't very many suicides. These meet weekly for six to eight weeks, and follow a structured agenda. They cover stages of grief, and seek to complete the cycle of grief. Open groups do not have programmed agendas, and meet regularly on fixed dates each month. At these groups, survivors deal with the problems they are experiencing at the time, and they have a mix of people close and faraway from the suicide. Group leaders are also survivors. They are very altruistic people who are through their grief and have a strong impulse to help others.

Dependency is a tendency to become unnaturally attached to a group, and some people worry this will happen with suicide survivors. Some open-ended groups are formed like clubs which one joins, as opposed to groups where people come together temporarily because of a common problem. There is nothing wrong with forming new friendships in a grief group, but it seems unwise to urge suicide survivors to join, and stay in a group for months and months — or years. To make a suicide death in your family the central focus of the rest of your life will take away necessary energy and attention that needs to be on you and your surviving family and friends.

Attend a group meeting as soon after the suicide as you can. The longer you flounder around trying to figure out what happened and what hit you, the more confused, helpless and hurt you will be. You may feel you just can't talk to a bunch of strangers, but take a deep breath and go.

You will meet role models. You will meet survivors who are further away from their loved one's suicide. You will see, for example, that they have gotten through the first six or nine months. You will also see and hear other recently bereaved survivors who are still reeling from shock and bewilderment as you are.

You may be shocked to discover that you are laughing in commiseration over some gross thing that happened. Early on in the grief group experience, you may need more from others than you can give. As you go on, you will find that you reach out to other people, because you have been there too. In rural areas or small towns, where there are no groups, suicide survivors can get together informally with newly bereaved suicide survivors. Ask your funeral director or pastor or rabbi if they know other suicide survivors who would get together with you. Other survivors can provide you with a measurement stick, a source of encouragement, and a haven for times of discouragement.

A suicide survivor's grief group is a supplement to one's natural support system; it is a temporary haven where a person can go to be with people who understand how they feel. You may feel freer to "let down" with other survivors than people close to you. The group is a place where you realize you are getting your own strength and confidence back to go on by yourself. Some survivors, after they are ready to leave the group, stay awhile longer to help newer people. A suicide survivor's grief group is one no one ever joins voluntarily, but it can be a lifeline to a future without someone you loved who died.

To say that grief is chaotic is to understate the problem. If only grief were a steady, upward progress from the death of your loved one to remembrance and renewal, it might not seem so bad. But grief is a period of falling down, picking yourself up, falling down, picking yourself up again — and again. As time passes, you won't fall down so far, and the times between falls begin to lengthen. But even still, it will not steady. Many people, around six or eight months after the suicide, have a setback. It *feels* like you are right back at the beginning, and that you've lost all the progress you thought you'd made. You haven't. You're human; you are healing. The other despairing times have passed, you have gone on, and you will again.

DO YOU NEED A PROFESSIONAL?

Most grieving people don't need professional help. They need support not therapy. If you do need therapy, there are many professionals available. You should see someone who practices psychotherapy or counseling, and many professionals do: psychologists, psychiatric nurses, social workers, and pastors are the most common. There are also grief counselors. Before going to any professional, check them out. This is not as difficult as it sounds. Ask someone you trust if they know of a good psychotherapist; more and more people are going to therapists for help with problems in their lives. There is very little stigma attached any more.

If there is a mental health clinic in your area, call it; it will have someone on its staff who can help you. (It also will have a psychiatrist in case you have depression.) Funeral homes sometimes have bereavement counselors. There are many resources. Whomever you go to, you should talk to personally first — either in person or over the phone. State simply what your situation is, and ask if they have had experience in helping grieving people. Good therapists will answer honestly, and if they don't have this kind of experience, they probably know someone they can refer you to.

You should know, however, that you will still have to do the work of grief. Psychotherapists are people who can help you with your problem; they do not solve it for you. Psychotherapy is talk-therapy, and you do most of it. Psychotherapy is rather like sitting and talking in front of someone while you talk and figure out solutions to your problem. The psychotherapist may guide you by asking questions or making occasional comments, but you do the work. What is the work of psychotherapy? It is to help you learn to think differently about your problems, and to look at new ways of solving them.

SOME HELPFUL CLICHES

A cliche is a truth that is so obvious, it sounds corny and old fashioned. Cliches are old truths — and they represent our legacy from all the collective wisdom of the past — put in a short phrase. One old cliche says: *Things turn out for the best.* That is not true in itself, but you can *make* things turn out for the best. Even though there are many things beyond our control in life, we are responsible for what is inside of us, and we have much more power to call on than we realize.

The great psychiatrist Victor Frankel says that the one thing no one can ever take from us is our *attitude* toward life. *We* are the ones who will decide how we look at the tragedy of the suicide in our lives; we *can* let it ruin the rest of our lives. We also can decide, as humans always have, that *we're not going to let this defeat us. Where there's life, there's hope.* One of the reason cliches like this are hackneyed sayings is because people have found them to be so true over the ages.

One of the tasks of grief is to regain your strength. Not only can you regain the strength you had before, but grief survived increases your inner strength. It may make you *sadder, but wiser;* enduring catastrophe taps that bit of extra strength you didn't know you had. Grief isn't solely related to death; it relates to all the losses we have in life. Each loss builds on the other, but the grief of death is the worst loss.

And the *first grief* for a person is worse than subsequent ones will be, because you have to go through it alone and discover your own guideposts. If your first real grief is a suicide, it may seem that you will never get over it. When you do, you may look back, with a justifiable pride, and wonder, "How did I ever get through it?"

One of the benefits of surviving an ordeal is that your added strength gives you more confidence. *If I survived this, I can survive anything!* you can say proudly. Suicide survivors not only get "through it," but can feel an extra pride of survivorship, because they not only survived the death, they did so even with all the extra problems created by the taboo and stigma on suicide. You can even feel a little bit superior about it. You've been *tested by fire.*

Another good that can come out of grief is your realization of how precious time is. *There's no time to waste,* our ancestors taught us. Now we know what they mean. Grief can teach us to *take time to smell the roses* and to value how important *now* is.

Cliches teach us that *there's no time like the present*. If we can learn to say those kind or loving words now — while we have the chance — we can avoid the kind of regrets we had for the things done and undone in the past. We can't do any more for someone we loved who died, but we can *make up for it* with the living. We may also need to learn that *all work, and no play, makes Jack a dull boy*. People in the past learned that workaholics lose out in life, or maybe we have not worked hard enough in the past, and need to *pull ourselves together* — we need to get organized.

There are any number of ways we may learn the wisdom of these ancient truths that are now cliches. Grief can teach us to *appreciate what we have* more, and to value what we have. Instead of yearning for what we can't have, we need to *take stock in ourselves*. We can look closely at our lives, and what is important and what we may have overlooked.

After a loss like a suicide death, you will find that just being alive is the basic value in life. There are all sorts of ways you can make changes in the quality of your life. But being alive is the *bottom line*. You need that first, and the lesson of grief is that when that's gone, you can't ever get it back on this earth. Grief teaches us that death is the one thing on earth that is irrevocable. One definition of spirituality is transcendence — to go beyond ourselves — beyond what we thought we were. This is one reason people sometimes become more deeply religious after a death; without realizing they could, they transcended themselves.

When will you "get over it?" When will you *be back on an even keel?* — back to your "new normal" again? Generally speaking, it takes time for a huge emotional wound to heal, and you need help. You may need to learn to ask for the help you need from the people around you. *I'll believe it when I see it,* you may be thinking, but you can and will.

We have the benefit of the ancient wisdom that tells us that *nothing new has happened under the sun. There are no new things; just the same old things happening to new people.* There have been suicides since men and women have been on earth. People survived then, and you will too. The future beckons to us, and we have a healthy impulse to return because of that "persistent breeze that blows towards us from the future." (Albert Camus.)

WORKING AT HAPPINESS

It sounds strange to say you must work at happiness, but what it means is that you should be good to yourselves and each other. Just because such a devastating thing as a suicide happened doesn't mean you shouldn't participate in enjoyable activities and can't have a small period of enjoyment.

There is no reason in the world that you cannot have the diversion of a movie, picnic, trip to the zoo, dinner out, or any other thing you normally enjoy. Yes, it will be bittersweet, and you may cry. So what? Getting back into life after suicide means getting back into your routine, which involves work, obligations, and things you enjoy.

Food won't taste good, your loss of concentration means you will miss half the movie, the sky will not be as blue, nor will the sun shine as warmly. But it will come. If anyone deserves the consolation of a bit of enjoyment, you do. The fact that you can laugh — even for a moment, or that you can divert yourself with a book for half an hour means you are going to be all right. It will take a long time and be hard, but you will be happy again. You have a right to recover from grief just as other people do.

THE FUTURE

Despite the low priority given to the problems surrounding suicide death, the future is bright. The progress made in the last half of the twentieth century in understanding the brain —how it works, how it gets sick, and how it gets well — cannot be turned back. The director of the National Institute of Mental Health said in 1990, that "90 percent of what we know about the brain was learned in the last ten years." There is a field called neuroscience that has made remarkable discoveries.

President Bush signed a proclamation making 1990 to 2000 "The Decade of the Brain." Congress has even increased appropriations for research. There is a strong commitment to research on major depression, manic-depression, schizophrenia and the anxiety diseases. We will also benefit from research that explores the organic things that go wrong in the brain, such as brain tumors and Alzheimer's disease. Scientists and pharmaceutical companies will continue developing medicines that are more effective, and have fewer side effects, for the treatment of mental illness. Families of individuals who have mental illness will begin to demand better educated psychiatrists, psychotherapists and other caregivers. Mental illness will be seen as the physical illness of the brain it really is. When people discover that antidepressants can take away the terrible emotional pain in two or three weeks, they will refuse to suffer a year and a half or more while their depression runs its course.

People won't stand for their loved ones suffering from untreated mental illness. They won't be silenced by the people who say it is all right to take medicine for physical illnesses, but people who have mental illnesses must suffer untreated, and pull themselves together by their own will. Suicide survivors banding together will be the new people who won't stand for being treated as outcasts because someone they loved died by suicide. Their friends and caregivers will become increasingly supportive. It's not fair, but only the families and loved ones of someone who died by suicide can banish the stigma; only those who wear the heavy cloak of stigma can throw it off. No more will suicide survivors be in the ridiculous position of not knowing someone they loved was sick until they died — by suicide. We must honor their memory.

The big "hot" topic of teenage suicide which surfaced will give way to a real concern and understanding of why *anyone* kills him or herself. And it won't just be teenagers that people care about — it will be all of the suicides. Suicide survivors aren't different from other people; they aren't saints, nor are they terrible sinners — just good people who have suffered a terrible tragedy: someone they loved has died. Only suicide survivors can say, "There was someone in our family who was very sick, and they died, and don't you dare try to place shame on their memory, or place blame on the family for their death." While grieving the past, a suicide survivor's task is to return to the future. All of history tells us that suicide survivors did because *they had to*.

Remember John? The man who had to to go school because he was the principal? You have to go on because you are the principal in your life. The work of your life is to rebuild after suicide. You always have two choices in life: you can quit or keep going. You know what will happen if you quit, but there is always promise and hope in the future. Things won't always go your way; you can't change the past, but you can take charge of your own life and make things "turn out for the best." You *have to* — because *you* are the principal of your life.

SUICIDE AWARENESS\VOICES OF EDUCATION (SA\VE)

In August 1989, thirty Minnesota suicide survivors met and agreed on the need for an organization. The task of forming one seemed overwhelming at the time, but they named it: Suicide Awareness\Voices of Education (SA\VE), and held a vigil in its name to honor the memory of people who died by suicide.

Six survivors worked on the vigil: Karen Deviny, Al and Mary Kluesner, Mary Swanson, Ben Van Sant and Adina Wrobleski. On April 28, 1990, 300 survivors gathered at the Minnesota State Capitol in St. Paul where the vigil was held and participants inscribed on a memorial wall the names of their loved ones who died. The experience of being together with so many other survivors was powerful, moving and energizing.

Having been so successful, they felt confident it was time to build SA\VE. In August 1990, six more Minnesotans joined the original six: Faye Bland, Reuel Nygaard, Bonnie Scherer, Nancy Theis, and Ron and Marian Weiss.

Education is the key word in SA\VE; and SA\VE will be the voice of suicide survivors. Survivors are studied and analyzed by "experts" who make dire predictions about them. They say one will never get over a suicide death or if by chance one does, it will take years. SA\VE feels survivors are the experts — they are the ones who know what it feels like to experience the suicide death of a loved one. They know they are good people, with no responsibility for the death, and others need to hear them.

SA\VE is different from the major mental health organizations: National Alliance for the Mentally Ill, National Mental Health Association, and the National Depressive and Manic Depressive Association. These are concerned with millions of sick people; SA\VE is concerned for the survivors of thousands of people who died by suicide.

The American Suicide Foundation and the American Association of Suicidology are concerned about survivors, but only at the grief and therapy level. The founders of SA\VE are *recovered survivors* who are working through education to prevent thousands upon thousands of suicides every year, a goal they know is possible to achieve.

The mission of SA\VE is to educate about suicide, and to speak for suicide survivors. The goals of SA\VE are:
- To educate about the brain diseases that, if untreated medically and psychologically, can result in suicide death.
- To make statements by their presence through staging events such as vigils and protests, by letter writing, and through other activities.
- To provide a network and organization for survivors for support and education.
- To honor the memory of their people who died by suicide.
- To eliminate the stigma on suicide.

As of this writing SA\VE has incorporated, held a second vigil and seeks members nationwide. For further information about SA\VE write: Adina Wrobleski, 5124 Grove Street, Minneapolis, MN 55436-2481 or telephone (612) 929-6448.

WHAT IS MAJOR DEPRESSION?

Depression is a brain disease in which the chemicals that affect how we think, feel and behave get out of balance. It is a state of constant, unrelieved misery. People who have depression often are angry and irritable. They often are dependent to a point of clinging to, and dragging down people near them. Sleep, appetite and sex are affected. They are unable to feel pleasure about anything. Unless the depression is recognized, it is very easy to dislike people who have depression, and blame them for things they can't control.

Major depression is a disease that goes away by itself in most people, but usually lasts for a year to a year-and-a-half, during which time there is immense suffering. Antidepressant medicines take away the painful symptoms in two to four weeks. The treatment for depression is medicine, psychotherapy or a combination of the two.

SYMPTOMS OF MAJOR DEPRESSION

The following is a list of symptoms of major depression seen in the at-large population and in young people. Some young people who have depression do not appear unhappy and sometimes look and are treated as if they simply have behavior problems.

SYMPTOMS OF MAJOR DEPRESSION	SYMPTOMS OF MAJOR DEPRESSION OFTEN SEEN IN YOUNG PEOPLE	
Obvious unhappiness	No apparent unhappiness	
	Defiance	
	Rebelliousness	Various
Inability to feel pleasure	Disobedience	Acting out
Preoccupation with sad thoughts	Running away	Behaviors
Crying and tearfulness	Drinking or on drugs	Commonly
	Refusing to go to school	Seen
	Failing in school	
Irritability and touchiness	Irritability and touchiness	
Feelings of helplessness worthlessness and hopelessness	Feelings of helplessness worthlessness and hopelessness	
Periods of withdrawal and isolation	Periods of withdrawal and isolation	
Loss of energy	Loss of energy	
Signs of self-neglect	Signs of self-neglect	
Loss of concentration	Loss of concentration	
Loss of interest in surroundings	Loss of interest in surroundings	
Loss of interest in favorite things	Loss of interest in favorite things	
Physical complaints (headaches, etc.)	Physical complaints (headaches, etc.)	
Sleep difficulties: insomnia or excessive sleeping	Sleep difficulties: insomnia or excessive sleeping	
Appetite difficulties: losing weight or overeating	Appetite difficulties: losing weight or overeating	
Loss of interest in sex	Loss of interest in sex	
Thoughts of suicide	Thoughts of suicide	

Not all people who have depression will have all of these symptoms, or to the same degree. If a person has four or more of these symptoms, if nothing can make them go away, and they last more than two weeks, he or she should see a psychiatrist, doctor or mental health professional.

CHAPTER REFERENCES

INTRODUCTION

1. Blumenthal SJ, Kupfer DK, NY Acad Sci 487:327-340, 1986.
2. Winokur, G, Clayton, P, *Medical Basis of Psychiatry,* 1986.
3. Andreasen, NC, *The Broken Brain,* 1986.
4. Roy, A. (Ed.) *Suicide* Asberg, M. et al, 1986.
5. Papolos, F. & J. *Overcoming Depression,* 1987.
6. Gold, M. *Good News about Panic, Anxiety & Phobias,* 1989.
7. Weissman M et al, New Eng J Medicine V321, N 18, 1989.
8. Blumenthal SJ, Medical Clinics of N America, V 72, N 4, July, 1988.
9. Robins E, Murphy GE, Am J Public Health 49:888-898, 1959.
10. Dorpat T, Ripley H: Comp Psychiatry 1:349-359, 1960.
11. Barraclough B, et al, Br J Psychiatry, 125:355-373, 1974.
12. Hagnell O, Rorsman B, Neuropsychobiology 6:319-332, 1980.
13. Blumenthal SJ, presented at the annual meeting of the American Psychiatric Association, Los Angeles, May 1984. 14. Robins E, *The Final Months,* New York, Oxford University Press, 1981.
14. Shaffer D, Gould M, Trautman P, Presented at the NY Acad Sci - NIMH Conference of the Psychobiology of Suicidal Behavior, New York, 9/85.
15. Shafii M, Carrigen S, Whittinghill JR, et al, Am J Psychiatry 142:1061-1064, 1989).

CHAPTER 1

1. New England J Medicine, 9/11/86.
2. New England J Medicine, 9/24/87.
3. Suicide & Life-Threatening Behavior, V 18(1), Spring, 1988.
4. American Journal of Psychiatry, 145:11, November, 1988.
5. The Journal of the American Medical Ass'n, V 262, No. 19,11/17/89.
6. Suicide and Life-Threatening Behavior, V 15, No. 2, Summer 1985.

CHAPTER 2

1. Caplan, PJ, Hall-McCorquodale, I. Am J of Orthopsychiatry 55(3), July 1985.
2. Anne Quindlen, Minneapolis Star Tribune, September 23, 1990.

CHAPTER 3

1. McIntosh, Death Studies, 12:21-39, 1988.
2. Wrobleski, Omega, V 15(2), 1984-85.
3. Wrobleski, Israel J of Psychiatry, V 24 N. 1-2, 1987.
4. vander Wal, Omega, V 20(2), 1989-90.
5. Barrett, T, Scott T, Suicide and Life-Threatening Behavior, 19(2), 1989.
6. Death Studies, V14, N5, 1990.

CHAPTER 5

1. Mark Solomon, excerpts from paper presented at the annual meeting of the American Association of Suicidology, April, 1985, Toronto.